Divine
Disenchantment

Divine Disenchantment

Deconverting from
New Religions

JANET LIEBMAN JACOBS

INDIANA UNIVERSITY PRESS
Bloomington and Indianapolis

Manufactured in the United States of America

Library of Congress Cataloging-in-Publication Data

Jacobs, Janet Liebman.
Divine disenchantment / Janet Liebman Jacobs.
p.   cm.
Bibliography: p.
Includes index.
ISBN 0-253-32396-7
1. Cults—Psychology.   2. Ex-cultists.   3. Charisma (Personality
trait)   4. Leadership—Religious aspects.   I. Title.
BP603.J3   1989

291.4'2'097309045—dc20   89-45192
                                                                CIP

1 2 3 4 5   94 93 92 91 90

For Gary, Jamie, and Michael

Contents

Tables

Figure

Acknowledgments

In looking back over the years of study and research which contributed to the development of this book, there are many people I would like to thank for their support, guidance, and insight. I am most grateful to James Downton who provided encouragement and inspiration throughout the duration of the project. I would also like to thank Michele Barale, Linda Ellis, Deborah Flick, Michele Simpson, and Marcia Westkott for their particular contributions to this work. Finally, I am deeply grateful to those individuals who participated in the study and who made this research possible through their willingness to share their lives and experiences with me. It is to the religious devotees—their joy, their pain, and their knowledge—that this work is truly indebted.

Divine
Disenchantment

that religious communities provide what Peter Berger has termed "mediating structures" (1979) between the privatized family and the public arena of employment and government. In contrast with this view, the theory proposed here suggests that religious movements, rather than being a means of transition between the private and public sectors of society, represent a different form of family life to which devotees become attached in their search for the American ideal.

For many of those who joined religious movements, their experience of childhood was tied to the family ideology that emerged out of the post–World War II period of prosperity and traditionalism. Within this cultural framework the family was idealized as the core of emotional life, a privatized world of loving relationships that shielded children from the harsh realities of the outside world. By definition this family ideal, internalized by a generation of children raised with the media images of *Father Knows Best* and other such paternalistic symbols, included only one form of kinship arrangements, the isolated nuclear family whose structure of patriarchal authority reflected the social norms and values of postwar America.

The family mythology of the 1950s and early 1960s laid the groundwork for the disillusionment that would follow for this generation of youth whose lives were often marked by the strain and conflict of family relations. The statistics on divorce, incest, battering, and child abuse reveal the underside of the patriarchal ideal, leading Jane Collier, Michelle Rosaldo, and Sylvia Yanagisako to conclude that "in our society the place where nurturance and noncontingent affection are supposed to be located is simultaneously the place where violence is most tolerated" (1982:36). The scholarship on the family that developed out of the reevaluation of American society after the 1960s (Sennett, 1970; Thorne, 1982) reveals the extent to which the family has been idealized in contemporary consciousness and the effect that such idealization has had on maintaining belief in the patriarchal system of family organization.

One manifestation of this strong adherence to family values was the proliferation of charismatic religious movements in the 1970s in which the religious community was portrayed as family and the charismatic leader as the divine patriarch.* Accordingly, a segment of disenchanted youth was drawn to these movements in search of the ideal family. Within this perspective, the idealization of the father in American society is of particular significance for understanding the nature of charisma in religious conversion. Feminist analysis of family structure has suggested that the gender-defined roles of traditional middle class families place women in the central role of socio-emotional development, while men assume the more external roles associated with income production, decision-making, and moral authority (Mitchell, 1974; Chodorow, 1974, 1978). The result of this sex-segregated division of labor within the family is the absence of the father from both the physical and emotional caretaking of children. This absence, Contratto (1982) argues, allows for heightened idealization which is often based on the real power and control that fathers exercise over family members. Thus, in assessing the impact of such idealization on daughters, Contratto concludes that because fathers are surrounded by "the halo of male power" they are unrealistically represented in the psychological lives of their children.

Mitchell (1974) elaborates further on the importance of the father ideal in the unconscious, as the father assumes a powerful symbolic presence which develops out of the cultural idealization of maleness in society and the actual power that men possess:

> In simpler words, every time a mother threatens her child with "I'll tell your father . . . he'll punish you," though she has in mind a real person and a real situation (which is by no means unimportant), it is to the symbolic father behind the actual father that her words refer. The dead father of the law, who alone can say, like the Judaic God, "I am who I am," is there,

---

*Not unlike mainstream denominations, the new religious movements have primarily been characterized by an authority structure in which men are more closely associated with God and hold positions of leadership and power within the organization. This is especially true for the larger charismatic movements such as the Unification Church, Divine Light Mission, and Krishna Consciousness, although many of the smaller groups reflect a similar patriarchal orientation as well. Even in those movements where women hold positions of power, for example, the millenarian cult studied in the early research of Lofland and Stark (1965), the concept of paternal divinity is frequently the predominant spiritual orientation espoused by the group.

however weak or absent his real representative may be, however dominant the mother, however apparently "matriarchal" the particular situation. (1973:394-95)

In the new religious movements, the person of the charismatic leader represents a merging of the human paternal ideal with the all-powerful God father described by Mitchell. The rise of charismatic religious movements thus can be understood as the desire to experience both the ideal family and the fathering of a protective and loving male authority figure. As such, the conversion phenomenon reflects the failure of the middle-class family to meet the needs of contemporary society (Jacobs, 1971) and the attending disillusionment with the nature of fathering in American culture. This failure has a gender focus as well in that many of the female converts, having been affected by the burgeoning women's movement and the rising feminist consciousness of the time period, sought a family alternative that maintained respect for women within a religious structure that valued female participation and the notion of women's spirituality. In this regard the new religious movements appeared to offer a promise of female equality and social acceptance.

The family ideal perspective on religious commitment may in part explain why new religious movements have been unable to attract individuals of color to any great extent. Archie Smith, Jr. (1978) has pointed out that the absence of black participation in the new religious consciousness reflects a failure of these movements to embrace the issues of racism and oppression in their ethical systems. Perhaps another factor that contributes to the insular quality of religious movements is the diversity of family arrangements that typify black culture, particularly with respect to the role that women assume within the black family (Anderson, 1987). Black women are often the heads of households as well as significant income providers. Thus, the idealization of the father may be more closely linked with the patriarchal structure of white middle-class families. Accordingly, the nature of idealism that characterizes the desire for religious community among white middle class adherents might be less relevant for youth whose primary relationships may develop within a more female-centered family structure.

Understanding the significance of idealism to the growth of alternative religious movements in the United States provides a starting point for the study of disaffection presented here. As commitment to new religions was characterized by the desire to attain an ideal, the problem of unmet expectations would inevitably arise for many of the new converts. This past decade has witnessed the results of such disappointment, as large numbers of devotees have left new religious movements, disillusioned with the social relations and sexism of group affiliation, the political maneuvers of religious bureaucracies, and the actions and betrayals of their spiritual mentors and teachers. Accordingly, the goal of this research has been to study the trend toward deconversion from religious movements and the process of disaffection whereby devotees break their social and emotional ties to a religious group that had once held the promise of salvation, both for this life and for life hereafter.

As a study of a process, the research presented here has both a descriptive and analytic component. From a descriptive standpoint, disaffection from religious groups is studied as an evolutionary phenomenon in which departure from the movement is carried out through a multistage process that has both a social and a psychological dimension. The nature of this process is then examined from the perspective of theoretical assumptions about social and emotional bonding and the way in which ties to social movements are formed, maintained, and finally weakened within the context of a religious organization.

The significance of this research lies in its contribution to the study of religious disaffection as a dynamic of social change. While a great deal of work has been done in the area of conversion theory, comparatively little research has focused on the phenomenon of deconversion and exit from religious movements. As such, the study presented here offers a view of deconversion which has, until now, received scant attention in the literature. Further, the findings of the research offer a new perspective by which to view the development of socio-emotional ties to religious groups. Such bonds are formed at three levels of the religious organization, the most significant level being that of the charismatic leader.

Although the importance of the charismatic leader has been recognized in studies of religious movements (Wallis, 1982), particularly as tragedies such as the Jonestown suicide pact highlight the destructive aspects of authoritarian control, the precise nature of the leader-follower relationship in small-group commitment has not been widely investigated from the social-psychological perspective. Thus, this study can contribute greatly to a further understanding of charismatic authority and the ways in which power-dependent relationships are formed. In addition, a feminist perspective has been brought to the analysis of data in order to clarify the ways in which patriarchal authority affects the conversion process and the definition of spirituality within the religious community. Finally, the study of deconversion provides a greater understanding of the meaning and importance of spiritual phenomena in contemporary life and the difficulties associated with separating from an intense religious involvement.

Background Research

Only recently has the phenomenon of deconversion been studied by sociologists and psychologists. As early as 1969, Armand Mauss presented an analysis of religious defection in which he developed a typology of disengagement from religious movements. According to this typology, exit from religious groups could be classified according to social, intellectual, and emotional defection. Although Mauss offered a starting point for analyzing the process of disaffection, little has been done in the application of his typology to alternative religious movements, with the exception of James Downton's work on Divine Light Mission. In *Sacred Journeys: The Conversion of Young Americans to Divine Light Mission* (1979), Downton devotes a chapter to disaffection from the religious movement, noting that in leaving Divine Light Mission devotees expressed disillusionment with the organization of the religious group (social defection) and with the ideological tenets of the belief system (intellectual defection). His findings suggested that further work was needed in the area of religious defection.

For the most part, the research on departure from religious movements has focused on deprogramming and forced exit from the group.

Ethical issues concerning coercion and questions of brainwashing and counterbrainwashing have dominated the field of religious deconversion. In this regard, Anthony and Robbins (1978) have addressed the moral implications of forced intervention to achieve defection, while assuming a highly critical view of the notion of religious conversion as mind control.

Others such as Byong-suh Kim (1979) have evaluated the trend toward deprogramming from a process orientation, arguing that through the experience of deprogramming, devotees are forced to interact with "significant others" in such a way as to alter their subjective reality with regard to belief in and affection for the group and its leadership. Thus, she explains deprogramming as the restructuring of social reality through the formation of a new ego identity for the devotee, as the former religious identity is negated.

In investigating the effects of such deprogramming efforts, Trudy Solomon (1981) conducted a study of 100 former members of the Unification Church to determine how different modes of leaving religious movements affected attitudes toward the religious group. She found that those who disaffiliate as a result of deprogramming are more likely to hold negative attitudes toward the group than those who leave voluntarily.

While interest in deprogramming remains high, the study of exit from religious movements has recently expanded to include the examination of religious disaffection as a matter of choice rather than coercion. Among the contributors to this field are L. Norman Skonovd (1981), Saul Levine (1984), and Stuart Wright (1983, 1984). In a study of defectors from the Unification Church and the Hare Krishna movement, Skonovd identified certain mechanisms (for example, exclusivity and ideological authoritarianism) that acted to sustain or to weaken commitment, and thus suggested it was possible to generalize about patterns of deconversion based on the shared experiences and perceptions of devotees. His conclusions laid the groundwork for a further sociological study of disaffection.

Levine, by comparison, takes a purely psychological approach to studying separation from religious groups. Rather than focusing on the structural factors that influence commitment, he views religious conversion as a radical departure in a path toward adulthood. According to Levine, joining and then leaving a religious group provides a "rehearsal" for the task of growing up. Based on a study of religious devotees over a 15-year period, Levine maintains that almost 90 percent of the religious converts to nontraditional religious movements will leave within two years of their commitment, as they mature within the context of the religious group, readying themselves for separation and adult status in the outside world. Levine, however, does not fully address the significance of the charismatic relationship to the conversion process.

Finally, Wright's research on religious defection takes a social-psychological view of changing commitment which more closely parallels the present study. Wright focused primarily on those factors that set the defection process in motion. He identified five factors that contribute to the likelihood of defection. These include:

> (1) the breakdown in member's insulation from the outside world; (2) unregulated development of dyadic relationships within the communal context; (3) perceived lack of success in achieving world transformation; (4) failure to meet affective needs of a primary group; and (5) inconsistencies between the actions of leaders and the ideals they symbolically represent. (1984:176)

In his evaluation of the impact of these five factors, Wright found that the leader's actions have the greatest influence in determining the likelihood of disaffection, a finding that is consistent with the results of this research and which will be further elaborated in the analysis of charismatic bonding.

Research Methodology

This study is based on an investigation of 40 former religious devotees. Each of the respondents had been a member of a religious movement and had left the group of his or her own volition following an intensive involvement with the religious community. The study was conducted on a voluntary basis by soliciting participation through newspaper advertisements and referrals. For the purposes of investigation, a definition of nontraditional religious movements was adapted from the work of Kim (1979). Religious movements were thus included which had the following attributes: the intensive search for a spiritual experience; the presence of a charismatic leader and a structured hierarchy of command; beliefs and rituals which deviate from conventional religious tradition; and a rigid discipline of behavior and devotion. In all cases, the religious movements were patriarchal in orientation and leadership.

Data were collected through the use of intensive interviews (see Appendix A for interview schedule) which lasted from one to four hours. The interview explored the devotee's initial involvement with the group, the process of conversion, and the social-psychological aspects of deconversion. In all but two cases, these interviews were taped and then transcribed as the analysis of data proceeded. In addition to the structured face-to-face interview, a brief written questionnaire (see Appendix B) was also administered in order to gather background information on religious upbringing, family history, and level of education.

With few exceptions, the interviews were conducted at the University of Colorado during a period of one year in 1982 and 1983. To minimize the problem of memory distortion and reconstruction, participants in the study were limited to those former converts who had left the movement within two years of their involvement in the research. Because of the intimate, personal, and frequently implicating nature of the study, great pains were taken in order to ensure anonymity and to reduce the possibility of identification. Therefore, in the analysis of data, group affiliation is sometimes intentionally vague in order to protect the privacy of the respondents.

The problem of anonymity, however, did affect the selectivity of the sample, in that fear of reprisal was a concern for at least four individuals who made initial contact with me but then refused to be interviewed or to further discuss their experience in the group. A second problem that emerged in identifying the sample was calls from religious groups, such as the Unification Church and the Way International, who had current members pose as disaffected devotees in order to ascertain the nature of the study and any threat the research might pose to their movements.

These difficulties notwithstanding, data gathering for the study was generally not problematic, as the geographic area (Boulder, Colorado) in which the study was conducted has been a mecca for alternative religious movements over the last two decades. As such, I found a diversity of disaffected devotees who were willing and often eager to share their experiences, honestly and openly, for the purposes of this investigation and for the personal value of recounting what had in many cases been a painful and emotional ordeal.

Sample Characteristics

The sample population for this study consists of 21 men (52%) and 19 women (48%). Other studies of religious groups (Wright, 1984; Bromley & Schupe, 1979) indicate a higher ratio of men to women, suggesting that these groups have greater appeal for males. This was not found to be the case among the respondents interviewed for this research. In keeping with other research findings, however, the respondents in the study are white (100%) and primarily from middle-class backgrounds (80%). The majority (69%) had attended some college either before entering the movement or while a member of the group.

One unique characteristic of this sample population is the diverse number of religious groups represented. For the most part, previous studies, including Wright's research (1983), have focused on either one group in particular or three or four of the larger movements such as the Hare Krishna sect, the Unification Church, and so on. By comparison, 16 different organizations are included in this study; a distribution of cases according to group and religious orientation is presented in Table 1. As this table indicates, the greatest concentration of respondents is in the Hindu-based groups (49.5%), with Divine Light Mission alone representing 22.5 percent of the sample population. Charismatic Christian groups comprise 25 percent of the sample, followed by the Buddhist movements (12.5%), and the followers of Reverend Moon and the Unification Church (10%).

The religious background of the former devotees showed a high number of Jewish (8) and Catholic (9) participants, and relatively few Christian fundamentalists (5). Overall, 38 percent of the sample reported that they had little or no religious training before entering the group. These findings lend some support to the view that religious converts who join nontraditional movements tend to have strong religious backgrounds. The average

TABLE 1

Religious Devotees by
Religious Group and Orientation

	Religious Group	Percent	Number
Charismatic	Church of Christ	10	4
Christian	Four Square Baptist	7.5	3
N = 10	Christian Fellowship	2.5	1
	Ecclesia	5	2
Hindu-	Divine Light Mission	22.5	9
based	Hare Krishna	10	4
groups	Sunburst	2.5	1
N = 20	Circle of Friends	2.5	1
	Rudrananda	2.5	1
	3HO (Healthy, Happy, Holy Organization)	7.5	3
Buddhist	Tibetan Buddhist	10	4
N = 5	Thai Buddhist	2.5	1
Other	Unification Church	10	4
N = 6	Bahai	5	2
	Total	100	40

age in which a respondent entered the religious movement was 23; the age span ranged from 19 years to 63 years of age. Over half the sample remained in the movement for four years or more with only three respondents affiliated for less than one year.

Although voluntary exit from the group was a criterion for inclusion in the study, two respondents were subjected to deprogramming efforts initiated by their families. In both cases, one a Hare Krishna devotee and the other a Divine Light disciple, the individual returned to the movement for a significant period of time after the deprogramming experience, maintaining that the coercive approach had not been effective and that the decision to leave six months or a year later came as a result of gradual disillusionment. Thus, both respondents were included in the study.

Finally, with respect to the selectivity of the sample, it should be noted that most of the individuals who participated in the study had experienced extreme dissatisfaction with the group and thus their view represents those devotees who were deeply troubled by their affiliation. The data therefore are not necessarily representative of those who might leave under less troubling circumstances. Nevertheless, the research suggests that deconversion, as it applies to the severing of all emotional, spiritual, and social ties to the group, can be studied as a phenomenon in which clearly identifiable patterns of disengagement are evident.

Theoretical Perspective

The overall framework for analysis presents a view in which alternative religious movements represent a religious form of family life. Within this perspective, the religious community is created and maintained through the development of surrogate family ties which are characterized by sibling-like associations among converts who enter into dependency relationships with the charismatic leader. This approach to the study of commitment and deconversion integrates two prevailing views of religious phenomena, the "quest for community" associated with the sociological interpretation of alternative movements (Robbins, Anthony, and Richardson, 1978) and the analysis of spirituality associated with the principles of ego psychology and object relations theory (Freud, 1950; Kohut, 1971; Pollock, 1975).

The merging of these two schools of thought emphasizes the importance of the relationship between social structure and the psychological dimensions of religion, as conversion and disaffection are experienced within a familial context that has as its goal the adoption of the charismatic leader as the symbol of the divine father. The theory elaborated here focuses on the parallels that can be drawn between patriarchal religious communities and patriarchal family relations. Each form of social life develops around the significance of paternal authority in the creation of emotional affiliations, belief systems, and the concepts of individual power and effectuality.

Chapter Overview

In order to provide a comprehensive view of the experience of commitment and disaffection, Chapter 2 presents three case studies, each of which follows a devotee through the stages of religious commitment beginning with initial involvement with the group, and culminating with the process of separation from the movement. The chapter concludes with a discussion of the differences as well as similarities in charismatic movements. Following the presentation of cases, Chapter 3 analyzes the nature of religious commitment from the perspective of family relations and socialization, a discussion which provides the background against which to assess the first stage of deconversion, the breaking of social ties to the religious community through challenges to authoritative control.

The second stage of deconversion is addressed in Chapter 4 through an analysis of charismatic bonding and the unconscious internalization of the leader as god or godly. This chapter focuses on the bonding that takes place between follower and charismatic leader, as this intense affective relationship defines the emotional climate around which religious conversion is initiated and sustained. The significance of gender to religious experience is elaborated through a discussion of sex differences in religious commitment and spiritual phenomena.

Chapter 5 extends the analysis of charismatic bonding to the social realm by exploring the conflicts which arise between the realities of religious life and the idealistic association of the leader with the divine. As such, the second stage of deconversion is presented as the disengagement from a deep emotional commitment to the charismatic leader and the rejection of his world view and definition of "truth."

The final phase of disaffection is investigated in Chapter 6 as former converts begin to redefine their social reality following the final break with the charismatic leader and the religious community he represents. In this section, the transitional phase of departure is examined as devotees experience a sense of loss, confusion, and disorientation once their identity is no longer defined by group membership. The reestablishment of social roots is then considered as these contribute to the creation of a new social reality. In the last chapter, a three-phase model of deconversion is elaborated. In this model, disengagement from religious movements is described in terms of stages of separation from the social organization and from the charismatic leader. The final stage of deconversion is then developed with respect to the reestablishment of outside ties and the former devotee's reintegration into external society.

2.

Change and Commitment

Three Case Studies of
Religious Disaffection

The following case studies are intended to provide a view of conversion and disaffection as experienced within three different religious orientations: Hinduism, Buddhism, and charismatic Christianity. Each case describes entry into the religious movement, the conditions under which membership in the movement was sustained, and the changes that led to disaffiliation from the group. The individual accounts of the conversion experience, based on the perceptions of the devotees, offer a comparative analysis that illustrates the gradual nature of disaffection and the evolutionary quality of deconversion.

Case 1. Mark and Sandy: The Premie Experience
in Divine Light Mission

In July 1972, Rapid City, South Dakota, experienced massive flooding. Mark had just been discharged from the military when he heard that they needed volunteers to help out with the clean-up. Within a few days of his discharge, he arrived at the flood site and immediately began work with the clean-up crews in the area. Among the debris and refuse of the flooded streets were pamphlets and leaflets that were being distributed by members of Divine Light Mission, the followers of the young Guru Maharaj Ji, who were called premies, which means "lovers of God."

Mark picked up one of the leaflets and read it. Something in the words of the Hindu teacher touched him and when a premie sought Mark out a few minutes later, he gladly returned with him to the ashram that had been set up after the flood. Four days later Mark left for Montrose, Colorado, a small mountain community where Guru Maharaj Ji was then headquartered.

In Montrose, Mark was initiated into Divine Light Mission, receiving Knowledge from the guru with a small number of other followers. Before his initiation he had always thought of himself as a Christian and had briefly considered joining the charismatic Children of God sect. But now in Colorado, in the presence of a young spiritual master, he believed he had found God. Here he describes his feelings after initiation.

> I was in this place where I was looking for the Lord to be on this planet. Maharaj Ji said accept knowledge and go on with your life so I did. I was really happy. To me the Lord was on the planet. Everything was going to be fine. I didn't have anything to worry about.

In the first year and a half that Mark was a premie he remained in Montrose. During this time he married Sandy, a young woman who was his neighbor in the mountain community. When he first met Sandy, she only vaguely knew what the Mission was about and who the young guru claimed to be. Before they married, however, she too received Knowledge, accepting Maharaj Ji as god on earth. Soon after their marriage, Mark and Sandy were transferred to Rapid City where Mark was given the position of representative for the Divine Light Information Center, while Sandy was given the responsibility of housemother in the local ashram.

In South Dakota their life as husband and wife centered around their spiritual practice and their respective duties in their service to the Mission. Sandy assumed all domestic responsibilities for the Information Center, while Mark took on the administration of the ashram and the recruitment of new members for the South Dakota district. In Rapid City, they lived among other premies, sharing meals and household maintenance, attending *satsang* (a daily meeting to share spiritual knowledge), and waiting for the next opportunity to see the Lord and to share in his vision for peace and happiness on earth.

Toward the beginning of Mark and Sandy's fourth year in Rapid City (1975), a change took place in the organization of the Mission. By this time the movement had grown very large with thousands of devotees forming a strong international following. Immense festivals were held every year, bringing premies from all over the world to gather quite literally at the feet of the spiritual master. At these festivals, Mark and Sandy found themselves among hordes of other followers, many of whom seemed to be more interested in fund-raising and money-making concerns than the more spiritual aspects of commitment. By 1976, it was clear that a schism was forming in the movement, creating a philosophical split among the premies who were the closest to Maharaj Ji in the Mission hierarchy.

On one side there were those high-status devotees who warned the young guru that he was in danger of becoming the kind of cult leader he had decried in other movements. These devotees encouraged Maharaj Ji to sponsor programs in which his divine right might be questioned. Thus, for a few months in 1976, such programs were initiated and Mark and Sandy attended discussion groups where the notion of total commitment was reassessed and questioned. Mark explained the change that was taking place in this way:

> At the time they started all these workshops, they were questioning-type workshops. Who was Guru Maharaj Ji? What is knowledge? We would get into these groups and try to solve it as a problem, using these problem-solving techniques. What began to happen was that Maharaj Ji began to lose people; premies were leaving the ashrams.

Aware of the declining number of devotees, a new power faction emerged within the movement which challenged the liberalization program. These members of the administrative hierarchy supported a more rigid and doctrinaire approach to conversion, and a return to the authoritative structure in which the Mission had thus far flourished in the United States. Maharaj Ji was also in favor of resuming a more orthodox stance and so less than six months after the liberalization effort had begun, the guru made a radio broadcast in which he reasserted his position as god on earth to his followers. Immediately following the broadcast, a nationwide reintensification program was begun. Mark and Sandy now found them-selves attending workshops that, instead of questioning the guru's deifi-cation, reaffirmed absolutely the godliness of Maharaj Ji.

Throughout the period of vacillation, Mark never stopped believing in Maharaj Ji. Whenever thoughts of doubt or negativity had entered his mind, he repeated Maharaj Ji's name over and over again to himself as he had been taught when he first took Knowledge, and with this chanting of Holy Name all doubt would vanish and reassurance and tranquility would return. The reintensification workshops helped to reinforce his faith. In the aftermath of the brief reformation period, the president of the Mission resigned and he and the other supporters of a more open approach to spirituality were labeled as heretics who had lost Maharaj Ji forever. According to Mark:

> Even when the workshops happened, it was just the subculture being exposed. Maharaj Ji was still the source of creation, the lord incarnate on the planet. He continued to be that way and what they said was that his detractors were *monmuts*; they had surrendered to their minds. A *monmut* means someone who has totally surrendered to his mind. And we weren't supposed to talk to them or have anything to do with them.

In the year following the reintensification movement (1977), Mark graduated from college in South Dakota. He and Sandy had a child now and they moved to Boulder, Colorado, to be near the Divine Light head-quarters in Denver, although Maharaj Ji was now living in Malibu, Califor-nia. Mark and Sandy stayed in Boulder for about a year and then moved to Montana to join a commune of premies who had established a new ashram in that state. Sandy had just given birth to another son and the family moved into a communal living space with fifteen other followers.

Under the more rigid regulations that had been initiated after the controversial year in the Mission, ashram life seemed harsh to both Sandy and Mark, but particularly to Sandy. Children were separated from their parents so that they would not interfere with the devotion of the adults. Family time was not encouraged; devotees were required to either take care of their ashram responsibilities or to participate in spiritual practice.

The person in charge of the Mission in Montana made it clear that the first priority of all premies was to serve Maharaj Ji, while children and spouses were relegated to a secondary place. The pressure that such demands placed on Sandy and Mark led to the first real test of their commitment. As ashram life became more unbearable, they suffered a great deal of emotional turmoil in trying to sort out and somehow allocate love for each other, for their two sons, and for Maharaj Ji as well. Finally, they made a decision to leave the Montana commune and move to California where they could live together as a family. At the time of this decision, they had been in the movement for seven years and they both feared that if they did not make the move, the pressures of ashram life would destroy the fragile family network they had established in spite of the demands of the religious life.

Just before moving to California, Mark and Sandy attended the annual festival of Divine Light Mission. Seeing Maharaj Ji once again, decked in flowers, awaiting the love and devotion of the premies, seemed to alleviate all the anxiety they had been feeling in Montana. When they kissed his feet and touched his robes it was as if they were young initiates again, receiving Knowledge and the Lord's love for the first time. In Maharaj Ji's presence at the festival, Mark felt as if he were entering a place of light where there was no one but himself and the spiritual teacher, a sensation of unification that had marked his first encounter with Maharaj Ji in Colorado. Experiencing once again this connection to the Lord, a feeling of wholeness and envelopment, he reaffirmed his commitment to Maharaj Ji, vowing, as he had during his initiation, to serve the Lord twenty-four hours a day, to follow all of his commandments, and to remember Holy Name always.

When the festival was over, Mark and Sandy moved with their two children to California where they lived by themselves for the first time since joining Divine Light Mission. Although they were no longer part of the ashram community, they felt renewed in their commitment, convinced that it had not been Maharaj Ji that created a crisis in their faith in Montana, but the other premies. Sandy explained the change she experienced:

I felt wonderful after we left Montana. And for the next year I couldn't be around premies. I couldn't go to *satsang*. It was the weirdest thing in the world. I was totally committed to Maharaj Ji, but I couldn't be with premies. To me there was a difference. You see, Maharaj Ji was clean and pure. Premies were this other thing, this organization that was its own entity. It wasn't until after I came out that I began to see that there was a definite connection between the organization and Maharaj Ji. He had created the whole thing. But in my mind I had separated them. I had to in order to keep the faith in Maharaj Ji.

Living independently, Mark and Sandy tried to establish a nuclear family lifestyle in which devotion to the Lord would be shared with devotion to family members. They rarely attended *satsang* or meditated on their own. After a year of living in this state of partial disaffection, they moved once again, this time to Ventura where there was no premie community at all. While in Ventura, Mark experienced a new crisis of faith as a result of a visit by Maharaj Ji:

The thing for me was that I felt like Maharaj Ji was the Lord and we were not obeying him. I started to feel real guilty. I went through that whole year without doing any meditation. I went to *satsang* twice during the whole time. We moved to Ventura and right after that Maharaj Ji came there. There was no community there and I thought in my brain, in my mind, he loves me. He is just coming here for me. I did, I believed it was all for me.

After that visit, all the guilt that Mark had felt for not attending *satsang*, for not faithfully performing his devotion, came over him in a wave of emotional intensity and he felt both elated at his special relationship to the Lord and distraught by the lack of faith he had shown in rejecting the premie life. A few weeks after the visit, Mark left his job and rededicated his life to Maharaj Ji, attending *satsang* once again every night and putting all his energy and time into the Mission.

Increasingly, their family life again centered around their devotion to the Lord and their intense feelings of love and commitment to Maharaj Ji. During this period, Mark and Sandy would fantasize and dream about visiting his mansion in Malibu with a hope of catching a glimpse of Maharaj Ji at home. That year, as the guru's birthday approached, Mark and Sandy found a special kind of film that they knew he wanted. Although all presents were to be delivered to Mission headquarters in Los Angeles, they decided to hand deliver the film to his estate in Malibu. On the day before his birthday, they drove up to the gates surrounding the guru's immense palatial home. Sandy described what she felt as they surveyed the huge stone walls:

> We heard through the grapevine that Guru Maharaj Ji really wanted this certain kind of film. We just thought this would be the perfect thing. It was from our hearts. We drove up to this mansion in Malibu and there were these big walls and just kind of subtly inside myself I felt like I was awed, but then I thought, for heaven's sake if the Lord were on the other side, why wouldn't he want to keep me out? It's just not practical for him to see thousands and thousands of people. We went up to the gates and that was as far as we got.

A few months later, Mark and Sandy left California and moved back to Colorado to be near former premie friends from earlier years of their membership in the Mission. In Colorado they reentered a communal lifestyle with other followers, devoting themselves to evening service and attendance at all devotee activities. Yet the more involved they became with the community, the more they felt a resurfacing of the tensions and anxiety they had experienced in Montana. The demands on the premies seemed endless. Now Maharaj Ji needed another new airplane, the jet they bought him last year was already inadequate. Two hundred thousand dollars had to be raised in a matter of weeks. Sandy and Mark and their two children joined the other premies in a massive fund-raising campaign during which all of their time and energy was spent in collecting money that was sent to California.

When Sandy complained to the local representative that devotion seemed to be measured according to one's ability to raise funds, she was told that a perfect devotee could show her love for the Lord through many forms of service and those who were lazy and unworthy were those who made false distinctions between spiritual devotion and other types of service to the one true Lord on the planet earth. Chastised for questioning the authority of Divine Light Mission, Sandy experienced pressure to be a perfect devotee, to give what was asked of her and her family without question or complaints, but her doubts about such demands she now kept to herself or shared in private moments with Mark.

After the massive fund-raising drive for the new plane for Maharaj Ji, it was rumored that the guru would be visiting the ashram in Boulder. Another fund-raising drive was immediately initiated in order to raise money for renovations that were necessary to accommodate the guru. For weeks Sandy and Mark, along with the other devotees, prepared the ashram for his visit, painting and building, preparing special meals, and redoing an entire room for Maharaj Ji. And then the day of his anticipated visit arrived. He was to come in the early evening, lead *satsang* for the community, take dinner with them, and then spend the night under their roof.

Sandy and Mark and the two children took great care over their dress and appearance for the visit, and they brought gifts that the family had made for the Lord, embroidered pillows and small carved objects. They arrived at the ashram at 5:30 that evening. Many of the premies were already waiting in the meditation hall, which had been strewn with flowers and smelled of burning incense. At 7:30 the tension among the devotees was high as whispers and sighs passed among the waiting disciples. His plane is delayed. He is on his way. His motorcade is stuck in traffic coming out of Denver. At 9:30, the group began to break up. The incense had all burned down and the flowers were beginning to wilt and droop. At midnight Mark and Sandy took their sleeping children home, while others waited until dawn the next day, still not convinced that Maharaj Ji was not coming.

In the morning Mark and Sandy returned to the ashram to help dismantle the festival decorations. A few of the premies still sat in the hall where they had spent the night, crying quietly to themselves. One irate young man shouted at Mark to leave the cascade of flowers that had been draped around a makeshift throne. "He is coming," he screamed at Mark. "Just leave everything alone." Later that day, the Boulder community called the Denver headquarters. The premies in charge said they knew nothing about the Boulder visit.

The disappointment Mark and Sandy felt after this incident heightened the sense of loss and betrayal that had begun to permeate their relationship to Maharaj Ji. In spite of a desire to remain devoted, it was increasingly difficult to ignore certain contradictions that were becoming apparent. Reluctantly Mark began to consider the terms under which love and devotion were demanded:

> I thought, this is a guru and he is supposed to love his disciples. And he is supposed to be a father to them and he lets rumors circulate about his presence to them, nothing factual, nothing practical, or considerate. People are waiting by the phone, is he coming, is he coming? No phone call but they are waiting. It struck me as a little crazy. Now there is a logical argument from Divine Light Mission, that it is a game. He wanted to see the commitment of his disciples. I can repeat the justification but I don't think that peace on earth would be manifest with people doing that to each other. To bring peace on earth you have to consider the mothers with crying babies, the people who have to wake up early and go to work; maybe you have to consider a lot of things.

In the nine years since Mark and Sandy had joined the movement, the organization had grown larger and more diverse and Maharaj Ji had grown more distant and inaccessible. Much of the time Mark and Sandy felt as if they were veterans among a group of new recruits who did not really understand the meaning of a true and loving relationship to Maharaj Ji. During this period of disillusionment, Mark thought back on the many festivals he had attended over the years. He tried to recall the feelings of light and love that images of the guru could sometimes engender. But more and more often his thoughts shifted to the many abuses he had witnessed, the times that Maharaj Ji had berated and humiliated disciples who were begging and pleading at his feet for a sign of love or a word of kindness. Such humiliations had always been excusable before; if Maharaj Ji treated his subjects in this way, there had to be a reason, part of God's plan for acknowledging his Being on earth.

Yet less and less were Mark and Sandy able to justify past abuses and the present sense of loss and hurt that they were experiencing. When their closest friends within the movement, the only premies to whom they still felt a bond, were kidnapped and deprogrammed in 1981, Mark and Sandy began to consider what had once been the unimaginable, that perhaps Maharaj Ji was not God, that perhaps they had been wrong in accepting the Indian teacher as the Lord incarnate on the planet. Such thoughts, which for nine years had been repressed at every suggestion of doubt, now forced their way into the consciousness of both Mark and Sandy.

With the support of their disaffected friends, they began to reevaluate all of their beliefs and actions that were associated with their commitment to Maharaj Ji. In doing so, they recognized that their connection to the movement had only survived because of their faith in the Lord. Ashram life, the majority of premies, and the Divine Light Mission organization itself had all, at one time or another, posed obstacles to their commitment to the guru. And now, when all of these barriers had been removed, there was only the relationship between God and his devotees to consider, and they could no longer chant themselves into believing that this relationship was fulfilling or satisfactory in ways that had been rewarding in the first few years of their involvement.

The more they talked to each other and the more they interacted with other former premies, the greater the doubts became until Mark finally acknowledged what had been perhaps his greatest fear, his desire to separate from Maharaj Ji. Letting go of the ideal love, the god figure to whom he had sacrificed much of his adult life, proved very difficult for Mark, in spite of the support that Sandy and his friends provided. He entered a deep depression. He could not work; he could not play with his children nor make love to Sandy. He tried to feel nothing at all rather than the overwhelming sense of anger, love, sadness, and loss that alternately created feelings of desire for Maharaj Ji and feelings of hatred for the guru.

To extricate Mark from this state of depression, Sandy contacted a counselor who dealt primarily with disaffected devotees. Together they attended a counseling session in which Mark recounted his experience, an emotional ordeal that released many of the feelings that he had wanted to repress. In the weeks following this first counseling session, he and Sandy continued to dialogue with each other, talking of nothing else but their experience and their feelings and beliefs with regard to the Mission and the guru who had so obsessed their lives.

Slowly, the intense feelings of anger and loss at being betrayed were replaced by a sense of freedom, an openness to thoughts and actions which had not been possible when Maharaj Ji had dominated all aspects of their consciousness. A simple experience like walking down the street took on new meaning. Mark could feel the warmth of the sun, experience that sensation, and his thoughts did not automatically revert to the guru as the source of all pleasure in life. For the first time since joining the movement in 1971, Mark experienced his feelings and his thoughts as his own. But such freedom was not without guilt as he thought of his betrayal in wanting to free himself from the "true path."

Although Mark and Sandy have completely disaffected, they still feel moments of anger when they regret all of the time that was wasted in ten years of devotion to a false god. Yet at other times a sense of doubt overtakes them and they wonder if they and their children will be left behind when Guru Maharaj Ji brings peace and love to the world. To cope with their spiritual loss, they now attend a small gathering of mystical Christians who meet weekly in the back room of a health food store in Denver. The group is led by an older woman who practices herbal medicine and spiritual healing which she ties to a belief in Jesus Christ. There are no rules or regulations imposed on those who attend the gatherings and membership in the group is open to anyone who wishes to attend. Like Sandy and Mark, many of the group members are disaffected devotees from other religious movements.

Both Mark and Sandy are more skeptical now. They do not believe in everything that their new spiritual teacher espouses. Still, they are attracted by her holistic approach to life, health, and spirit, and they are soothed by her soft exhortations to find the truth within. For now, at least, Mark and Sandy feel as if they have "come home" again, that their belief in God has found a familiar voice in the prayers and wisdom of a soft-spoken Christian healer.

Case 2. Kathy: a Buddhist Disciple

In 1971 a small Buddhist community was established in a rural area of New Hampshire. The community was led by a spiritual master from Tibet who had recently come to the United States where he had gained a small following of devoted Buddhist converts. Among these was Kathy, a young woman from Nebraska who had just graduated from college. Her lover had gone to India to study under another Buddhist master and she had come to the ashram in New Hampshire in search of a connection to her former lover:

> I was looking for Buddhists in some way because the man I cared deeply for was studying Buddhism in India. There was a little tiny announcement at the local grocery store which invited everyone to an open house at the Buddhist monastery. It was a farm, a quickly put together commune with a big circus tent in the backyard for talks. I met His Holiness the first weekend I was there. But it was not because of him that I stayed at first but because I wanted to deepen myself, to be closer spiritually to the man I cared so deeply for.

As a new member of the monastery, Kathy began her Buddhist studies under the Tibetan Master, Karmapa. From the outset of her involvement with the group, she was taught the need to "forsake one's existence for the sake of another being," to travel on the path toward enlightenment by giving up her ego to the spiritual teacher. The focus of her commitment thus became to surrender herself completely to the guru in order to attain a higher level of spiritual awareness. To this end, she meditated for at least four hours a day under the strict tutelage of Karmapa who encouraged his disciples to lay bare their emotions, to delve into the innermost recesses of their consciousness through meditation, and to find the god within through their devotion to the teacher.

Kathy proved to be a very dedicated disciple; she practiced her devotion faithfully and became well schooled in the Buddhist teachings. Within two years of her association with the movement, she thought she might be considered for a teaching position, but her status within the community was never quite secure. The more she studied and meditated, the more she found that all of her thoughts and feelings were somehow tied to the guru. When she was away from him, he was always in her consciousness and when she was in his presence, she felt somewhat helpless, as if she could not defend herself against the emotional upheaval that his godliness engendered in her.

As her feelings for Karmapa become more intense, she began to experience a sense of alienation from the other devotees who surrounded him with obedience and devotion. Her relationships within the movement were primarily limited to a few women friends and a man who had become her lover. After a year or two at the rural monastery in New England, the growing Buddhist community moved to a more cosmopolitan university town in the West where Kathy's relations with the other community members grew even more strained. By now there was a well-established hierarchy of enlightened devotees from which Kathy was excluded and thus her need for Karmapa received little support from those who were closest to him.

In 1974, Kathy moved with her lover to an apartment in the meditation hall that the movement had purchased. By this time Karmapa had a following of about 500 in the West and living space was allocated sparingly to those who served the Buddhist community most faithfully. Kathy and her lover were among his early followers and thus they received living space in the coveted meditation building. At this point in her commitment, Kathy was practicing her meditation at least five hours daily and still hoped to obtain a teaching position in the movement. Her hopes, however, were shattered when she became pregnant.

Although Kathy believed that her lover had wanted her to bear his child, he refused to accept the responsibility. When she told him that she was pregnant, he requested a private audience with Karmapa. A day or two later, Kathy was called in to see the guru. At this interview, she was told that she could have the child, but that she was to go on welfare. Her lover had requested that he be sent to a different community in another part of the country and Karmapa agreed that this would be the best course of action for them both. Kathy was devastated.

> I was traumatized by the fact that I was being deserted while I was pregnant. I didn't want to marry him. But he told me he wanted to have my child. It was not an accident. What I did want was financial and emotional support which seemed to be only a human response. Because I was so traumatized, the situation escalated and the community never responded with any kind of warmth or understanding. They told me I had done it to myself. They took advantage of my vulnerability and turned it into a nightmare.

After the interview with Karmapa, Kathy's lover moved away and she did not see him again for a number of years. When he left she was forced to vacate the apartment next to the meditation hall. The administrative hierarchy told her that she could stay in community housing but that she should move in with another woman who at the time was in an intimate relationship with the guru. Pregnant, and feeling isolated by her desertion, Kathy found living with Karmapa's lover quite difficult.

The sexual aspects of commitment had always been a problem for Kathy. When she first joined the movement at the monastery in New Hampshire, she had been asked to stay with Karmapa in his small cluster of rooms. It was made clear then that if she stayed with him she would be expected to cater to his sexual needs, that such service would be honorable for a female devotee. Despite the pressure to have sexual relations with the guru, Kathy had declined to engage in this type of relationship with him, hoping that her path could remain purely spiritual.

Being forced to share an apartment with one of his many lovers brought the issue to the surface once again for Kathy who was still struggling with the tie she felt to Karmapa and her desire for a spiritual life. When Kathy refused to encourage or condone the sexual liaison between her roommate and Karmapa, she was asked to leave this woman's home. News spread quickly among community members and Kathy spoke openly about the way she had been treated because of her pregnancy and about her feelings concerning the sexual demands of commitment. She told other group members that she thought she had been punished for refusing to have sexual relations with Karmapa.

Kathy spent the remainder of her pregnancy in a Buddhist dormitory among the more transient community members with whom she had little in common. After the birth of her son, she was permitted to relocate to another Buddhist household that was composed primarily of older members of the community. There she recovered from a difficult birth and delivery, and when she became physically strong enough, she once again began to meditate many hours a day, seeking an audience with Karmapa whenever possible. When the guru agreed to see her, he often berated her, reminding Kathy of her weakness and egocentricity. Yet in spite of his attitude toward her and the alienation and loneliness she experienced within the movement, she would not hold him responsible for the actions of his followers and she could not envision a life in which her teacher was not intricately involved.

When Kathy's child was a year and a half old, she developed a friendship with one of the men in the community who would visit her nightly. For the most part they talked about their Buddhist studies and they meditated together, their intimacy limited to that of a trusting platonic relationship. One night, however, he suggested that their friendship become more sexual, that they become lovers. At first Kathy hesitated. At this point in her life and her involvement with the community, she was fearful both of an emotional commitment and of the physical aspects of a sexual relationship. But after a week or so of coaxing, this man came to her apartment quite drunk and began to coerce her. Although she felt sexually compromised, Kathy had relations with him which she found very painful.

Almost immediately, this devotee became more demanding of her sexually. He expected her to have relations with him every night and he told her that Karmapa knew of his expectations and encouraged him. With the support of the guru and with the memory of the disdain with which she had been held in the community when she refused to acquiesce, Kathy felt she had little choice but to enter into a relationship with this devotee:

> I went ahead and lived with him and when I could not perform sexually for him every night I was beaten. His Holiness knew of the physical abuse and sanctioned it. He told the man who beat me up that it was okay. He gave him comfort and had private talks with him. Finally I said I had had enough. I was not going to mount the guru's routines any more. What I objected to was the chauvinism and when I spoke out, I was physically threatened and told to keep quiet.
>
> Finally, I confronted Karmapa at a big community wedding. I spoke openly and frankly about what I thought. He rejected me as a student then, but I still couldn't leave. I still felt enclosed by him.

After confronting the guru publicly, Kathy requested an audience with another Buddhist teacher who was visiting the United States as a guest of the numerous communities around the country. Kathy explained her position to this visiting scholar. She made it clear that she wished to leave her guru but to continue her Buddhist studies and she was unsure how to separate from Karmapa and continue on a spiritual path.

The visiting Buddhist dignitary told Kathy she could continue her studies but that she should find another teacher among the other scholars who resided in the United States. He advised her to leave the Buddhist community where she experienced so much conflict. Taking this advice, Kathy moved out of the house in which she had been living, and left a message at community headquarters that she was officially leaving the Karmapa movement after seven years of struggle:

> I took refuge with two different Buddhist sects then and I made it clear that my purpose in seeking them out was to protect myself from any further harm either spiritually or psychologically. People had threatened me because they were afraid I would speak out about my experiences. Between 1976 and 1978 there was a period where I was trying to reconstruct my own life with the help of the other gurus and also some therapy as well. By 1978 I could finally say openly and without fear that anyone wishing to leave His Holiness Karmapa and reenter the real world would find it very difficult because that sense of themselves which was broken down would no longer be functioning.

After remaining for some time with the other sects, Kathy eventually returned to the university town where the Buddhist community had firmly established itself as a significant part of the cultural and religious environment in that area of the country. Since 1980 she has lived there with her son, although her relations with the movement remain strained. For the most part, other Buddhists refer to her as a "bit insane," a neurotic who brought all her grief upon herself. In spite of the disdain with which she is held by the group, Kathy remains in close proximity to her former guru, unable to make a home for herself anywhere else. Her parents, a wealthy Midwestern family, reside in a nearby state; but they have sustained only minimal contact with their daughter since her conversion in 1971.

Although Kathy still speaks of Karmapa as a holy man, she has found another teacher to whom she has transferred her devotion and love. Her new guru is a Hindu master who offers a less authoritarian spiritual path. Aware of the pain of her former affiliation, she believes that the new teacher will never allow her to have an expectation that he cannot fulfill. In looking toward her future spiritual life, Kathy reassesses the past in light of her experience:

> I realize now that I had to lose my enlightenment to regain it. I had to experience being around immoral people because I had never experienced that before. It's really the classic story of the little girl from the Midwest who goes to Greenwich Village. It is exactly the same process.
>
> I wondered why I had been brought into this high spiritual level to be brought down to this debased existence. Living in a spiritual world in your mind while living in a subcivilized culture in your life points to the tremendous hunger that is going on in many of us today for freedom, the tendency we have to keep ourselves in bondage while longing for freedom.
>
> I have never stopped meditating; I have never stopped developing my spiritual side. I'm just one of these beings who will keep doing it, no matter what happens in my life.

Case 3. Ted: A Devotee of Christian Fellowship

Compassion Hills is a Christian Fellowship Community located in the foothills of Colorado. The Fellowship is headed by Pastor John who founded the communal farm and bakery in 1972. At that time, most of his followers were drawn from the nearby university campus where Pastor John would preach daily, exhorting the students to find God and to take Jesus into their lives. Those who listened to his message were encouraged to give up their possessions, sever all ties with friends and family, and to participate in a Christian way of life that could provide for all their needs.

Ted arrived at the farm in 1980, almost eight years after it had been established. There were 120 followers living at the farm then, a number that far exceeded the thirty-five initial devotees who had made their home with Pastor John in the early 1970s, living in tents on the 100 acres he had purchased in rural Colorado. By the time Ted joined the Fellowship, there were three permanent dormitories, one for men, one for women, and one for married couples. The farm was flourishing and Compassion Hills pies and cookies were being sold all over the Western region. Ted, like the other members, received food, shelter, and $125 every three months in return for his labor. Life in the Fellowship centered around the operation of the farm and bakery, the profits from which were used to maintain a missionary program overseas.

The religious and social aspects of community life were controlled by Pastor John. He permitted little fraternizing among the men and women at the farm and enforced a rigorous daily schedule for his devotees. Work in the fields, primarily done by the men, and work in the bakery, primarily done by the women, began at sunrise, while prayer meetings were held promptly at sunset. All other time was allocated to the study of the Bible in preparation for the missionary work for which the followers were being trained. Pastor John was a strict disciplinarian who insisted on publicly admonishing disciples who broke the rules or who were lax in their responsibilities. It was therefore not uncommon for Ted to witness the public spanking of a child who had misbehaved or the communal condemnation of a young woman accused of sexual misconduct.

From the beginning of his association with the Fellowship, Ted enjoyed a close relationship with Pastor John. He moved to the farm after two years of junior college and almost immediately assumed a position of manager, overseeing the other laborers. Ted had first become acquainted with Compassion Hills through an old family friend who had been like a father to him and who had recently joined the Fellowship to help in the administrative operation of the growing community:

> Dad left home when I was in seventh grade and that was when I became born again because of the Johnson family. My best friend was Terry Johnson and his father, Bob Johnson, was a pastor in a church. I attended church with them and Bible study throughout high school. When they told me about the farm I wanted to see what it was like. I got to know Pastor John and he offered me this position there. He certainly appeared to be a man of God so I thought I would try it. That way I could be near Mr. Johnson too. I saw it as a very positive thing.

Ted quickly became acclimated to the structured lifestyle at Compassion Hills. He enjoyed the regimentation and he studied very hard,

hoping to obtain a missionary assignment within a few months. For the
first time in his life all his energies were devoted to a spiritual existence,
through service to Pastor John and to God, and he felt very at home
among the other devotees who had also dedicated themselves to a Christian fellowship. Within just a few months, however, life at Compassion
Hills changed, as Bob Johnson and his family took on a more important
and obvious function in the running of the farm.

Johnson had first been invited to join Compassion Hills when the
pastor discovered that he had a heart condition. He wanted someone
who could replace him eventually as the leader of the Fellowship and he
told his disciples that in his prayers and in his private moments with God
he had been directed to Bob Johnson, a pastor in a small church in Denver. In the first six weeks that Ted was at Compassion Hills, Johnson
began a reorganization of the bakery and farm in order to improve their
productivity. To this end, he appointed a Table of Advisors, a governing
board of Christian leaders from fellowships throughout the country. In
establishing the advisory board, Johnson included others in the planning
of goals and objectives for the missionary Fellowship and in the examination of financial reports and productivity schedules for the business operations. Prior to this time, only Pastor John had been involved in the
dealings of the farm in this way.

Further, Johnson included Ted in two other plans for change that he
had devised. The first was to improve the Fellowship's relations with the
nearby farm community by sponsoring work efforts and social events
that would bring the two communities together. The second was to enlist
Ted's help in encouraging other disciples to resume contact with their
families outside the movement. All these changes were done in rapid succession of one another within the first year that both Johnson and Ted
were in the Fellowship.

The other responsibilities that Johnson assumed focused on the missionary program. In order to ensure that everything ran smoothly in Africa and other areas where the Fellowship had been established, he was
often away from the farm for long periods of time, leaving Ted to help
Pastor John implement the reorganization efforts. During the weeks
when Johnson was away, Ted became quite close with the Pastor who

repeatedly told Ted how important he was to the Fellowship and how much he valued the hard work that he had thus far given to the farm.

When Ted had been at Compassion Hills for six months, Pastor John called a community meeting one evening after work. Johnson was out of the country at the time, although his wife and two children were living on the farm in a large house they had built with the savings they had brought to the Fellowship. At this meeting, the Pastor told his followers that "the devil's cloak of evil had been drawn over his eyes." He looked directly at Ted as he spoke to the others and said: "I don't think that was of God when I said it was time for Mr. Johnson. I have prayed more about it and I think I was misled by the devil in bringing him here." Then Pastor John berated the Johnson family, specifically pointing to Johnson's wife, accusing her of seductive behavior and sexual misconduct in general. A week later he dismissed the Table of Advisors, explaining to Ted that he did not want their input anymore:

> I guess he had a change of heart. Pastor John told me he didn't need them. He said he was disassociating himself from them and that they were no longer his advisors. "I run Compassion Hills," he said, "there is no one else."

The pastor told Ted that he thought that Johnson and his family had come under the guise of the devil but that Ted was not to be condemned for being misled, as the pastor himself had been misled. He wanted Ted to stay at Compassion Hills and to continue with the managerial work in which he had proved himself so capable. Johnson, meanwhile, had returned from Africa. Having learned of the pastor's actions from the advisory board, he stayed at the farm only long enough to pack up his family and move to the nearby town, leaving his home and furnishings behind. Johnson's sudden departure and the bitter acrimony that developed between him and the pastor left Ted in a confused and ambiguous position between two men that he had grown to love, one as a surrogate father and the other as a surrogate god:

> It was hard for me because I would go and talk to Pastor John and he would encourage me to stay on the farm. And I had a lot of respect for him and I believed that he was directed by the spirit of God. But then Mr.

Johnson said he thought that Pastor John was not a man of God, that he might even be a little shady. After they left, the Johnsons found out that Pastor John had been married twice and that he had been ordained as a pastor through the mail. I had always listened to Mr. Johnson and I figured he wouldn't feel this way about Pastor John unless there was a good reason. But still I had a hard time accepting a lot of things they said about him. No, not Pastor John, I just couldn't get that feeling about him.

After Johnson left Compassion Hills, the farm went into a state of physical turmoil and spiritual crisis; more than half the Followers left the fellowship as a result of the altercation between Johnson and the pastor. Ted, however, did not leave immediately. Although he had come to the Fellowship primarily because of his relationship with the Johnson family, once in the movement he had developed a strong and spiritual tie to Pastor John who, in Ted's perception, had perhaps erred but had not relinquished his place as Jesus' emissary. When, however, only forty devotees remained at Compassion Hills, Ted reluctantly left as well, deciding to return to school rather than continue with his missionary training. In the aftermath of his painful separation from the pastor, Ted enrolled at the university and immediately tried to establish contact with other Christians:

> When I first got back I started an informal get-together among people I knew. A lot of my old friends came who knew I had been to Compassion Hills. A lot asked me how it was. I had been the only one who had taken the departure to a fellowship like the farm. There was a group of about five of us who came to meet about once a week. We got a little Bible study going but it didn't really last too long because everyone got busy with school.

Disappointed with other Christians who had not known a total commitment like that of Compassion Hills, Ted missed Pastor John and life at the farm far more than he had anticipated. For a while, he tried leading a church youth group but quarreled with the administration over the lack of emphasis on spiritual training for the teenagers. He also attended a few meetings of the Church of Christ, a charismatic movement that was strong among his university peers. But this association he found particularly dissatisfying:

I see the Church of Christ as a cult. They have this thing called testimony. The idea is that you stand up in front of a congregation and say, "I have saved two people today." I want to say, really, how did you save them? I went to church there. Their definition of saving is how many people you can get to pray with you, to say they have accepted Jesus Christ, and that is not my attitude. No one has the right to save other people. That is not what the church is set up to do. Maybe it is God's will that the Church of Christ is ordained to do that but I don't know. I don't think that I know more than anyone else and I would be real skeptical of anyone who says they do and they can save you.

After suffering the disappointments of the religious life available to him at the university, Ted returned to the small church in Denver where Bob Johnson had once again assumed a position of elder and part-time pastor. Although Ted has chosen to stay with his first spiritual mentor, he is still unsure about the way God intervenes in one's life and what the meaning of his love for Pastor John has meant. He, however, is certain that God does intervene in very concrete ways, such as the calling that Pastor John received to do the Lord's work through Compassion Hills.

Because of his early conversion with the Johnson family and his later commitment to Pastor John, Ted believes strongly in his special relationship to Jesus and regrets that he has not yet learned to use the knowledge that God has given him. Although he is continuing with his university education, he is waiting for a direction from God that will help him to realize the missionary goal he had set for himself through his work with Pastor John.

Emerging Patterns of Deconversion

The case studies illustrate the lengthy and often difficult stages a religious convert passes through as he or she enters and leaves a religious movement in which a complete world view and theology have been adopted, practiced fervently, and then ultimately rejected. Whether the group is a large bureaucratic organization like the Divine Light Mission or a small religious commune like the Christian fellowship, the devotee is confronted with similar moral and ethical dilemmas as questions of truth and deception merge in life experiences focused around a belief in one true path to God and salvation.

In choosing to leave the religious movement, devotees attempt to resolve their conflicts through a separation process that involves both a social and psychological exit from the group. A pattern of defection thus emerges that forms the basis for developing a model of deconversion in keeping with Mauss's (1969) distinction between states of partial and total disaffection. In the chapters which follow, this model will be elaborated, beginning with a discussion of social departure from the group. The first stage of defection, social exit from the religious movement, represents a state of partial deconversion and lays the groundwork for the more difficult task of psychological disengagement from the charismatic leader.

3.

Rejecting the World of Total Meaning

Social Departure from the Religious Movement

In an essay on contemporary cult religions, Bucher (1983:279) describes current religious phenomena as "worlds of total meaning" that have a far-reaching impact on those who become converts:

> Those who enter the world of the Unification Church, People's Temple, Krishna Consciousness, the Children of God, Divine Light Mission, etc., often have received a new identity, name, clothing, language, ethical codes, friends, and a community. They receive a new religion, ritual, sacred literature, doctrine, a source of authority, and a mission. They also inherit a new world view; interpretations of the past and future, of the world outside, of their parents, of their purpose in the world, and of what is right and wrong with culture as we know it. This totally prepared, orderly reliable complex of ritual, symbol, myth, belief, doctrine, and relationship is a world of total meaning.

As this new world of total meaning comes to define the life of the religious convert, the devotee is engaged in a process of resocialization whereby a new subjective reality is created through the interaction with the social stimuli of the religious environment (Berger & Luckmann, 1966). In charismatic groups these social stimuli take the form of ideological indoctrination and spiritual practices that are geared toward the development of a religious family consciousness that replaces the family of

39

origin as the source of needs gratification. The conversion strategies employed by the movements, including prayers, chanting, meditation, and visioning, create primary associations for the convert which result in the formation of social bonds to the group and deep emotional ties to the charismatic leader. Thus, as Marx and Ellison suggest, religious groups "resocialize the individual away from familial norms and values, wean him away from dependence on the nuclear family" (1975:52), while establishing new dependencies on the religious community.*

The Unification Church, for example, uses a family-centered approach to religious indoctrination, as the following account by Edwards describes:

> Unification Church recruiters frequently give a selective view of their lives and a limited or deceptive view of their current religious affiliation to initiates, a faithful practice called "Heavenly Deception." If the recruiter can paint a selective portrait of himself (based on information given to him by the initiate) which appeals to early childhood experience of the initiate, the recruiter can exert control over the interaction in a pattern similar to the initiate's early relationship to a parent or older sibling.
>
> This practice of appealing to early childhood experience in a deliberate manner can achieve remarkable effects. After a week-end with the group, for example, I experienced a visual resemblance between my recruiter and my father. Different members of the group looked and acted like significant people from my childhood—my mother, grandmother, and brother. As a movement recruiter I noticed that my practice of these strategies could rapidly bring initiates to a similar state of mind. Group members tacitly acknowledge and reinforce these tactics at group meetings where discussions about various new spiritual children are held. . . .

---

*The means through which religious groups resocialize potential converts and thus modify subjective reality have been the subject of numerous controversies concerning questions of brainwashing and mind control. Conway and Siegelman (1978), for example, take the view that converts to nontraditional religious movements are coerced into commitment through brutality and force and therefore lose their ability to judge or make decisions for themselves. In contrast to this "brain-washing" perspective, other researchers such as Lofland and Stark (1965) and Levine (1984) maintain that religious commitment is a matter of choice on the part of devotees who assume a religious problem-solving approach to life. The findings of this research strongly favor the voluntary character of religious commitment and the view that conversion represents a rational life choice for individuals seeking social affiliations, control over their lives, and spiritual growth.

Group life reflects the religious belief that individuals enter a spiritual hierarchy by becoming children, siblings and eventually parents to other spiritual children as they reach a state of perfect identity with Reverend Moon and God. These roles are constantly opposed to the roles converts have experienced during their "fallen" lives. Physical parents, siblings, and their previous childhood roles are disparagingly compared to the simple, perfect, spiritual order. Group members learn to idealize their new spiritual family members, expecting the fulfillment of childhood desires for affection without the pain of separation. (1982:33-37)

As conversion is experienced within this idealized context, deconversion signifies the failure of the religious community to fulfill the promise of the world of total meaning. As life within the religious family unfolds, the newly formed bonds of affiliation among devotees are weakened by conflicts that arise over issues of power, authority, and control. Such conflicts often assume the character of sibling rivalry as the structure of the movement influences the strength of social ties to the group and the viability of the new social identity created through the conversion experience.

The Effects of Structural Arrangements on Religious Disaffection

All of the nontraditional religious groups included in this study have a strong authoritarian structure in common, with the charismatic leader at the apex of a religious organization that has a defined, hierarchical order. In only the smallest groups did this hierarchy consist of just two strata, the leader and his followers. For the most part, the majority of religious movements can be characterized as large extended family networks in which a three-tier power structure exists. At the base of the hierarchy are the "ordinary" followers who have little status within the group. At the middle level are a cadre of higher-status devotees who are directly responsible to the leader, the dominant figure who maintains ultimate power over the operations and spiritual life of the religious community.

The distinction among the levels of organization is important in that disillusionment with the group is at first focused on the middle-level leadership (the higher-status "siblings") who represent a separate sphere of authority apart from the charismatic leader. As such, these high-status devotees, the initiators of Divine Light Mission, the Vajra directors among the Buddhist sects, and the church elders in the charismatic groups, act to separate the leader from the lower-level devotees and to create a social distance by which the charismatic founder is removed from the more mundane aspects of community life. The challenges to authority that arise within the religious family are thus directed at those who occupy an intermediary position between the followers and the charismatic figure.

The higher-level devotees derive their authority from a seniority system in which specially selected disciples with ties closest to the leader, like the older siblings within a family, are accorded the deference of a privileged class of followers. Within the religious communities, the subordinate level of leadership is responsible for maintaining obedience to rules and regulations and for controlling access to the spiritual leader. The first stages of disillusionment are thus characterized by conflicts which develop around issues of status and the regulation of social and spiritual behavior. With the growth and expansion of religious movements, these conflicts are intensified, as the case studies suggest, by the changes in the structure of community life that result in the bureaucratization of the religious organization. Table 2 indicates the four most significant areas of dissatisfaction reported by the devotees. As this table indicates, control over the regulation of social life is by far the greatest source of disillusionment and that realm of commitment where challenges to the normative structure of the religious family emerge first.

The Regulation of Social Life

Seventy-five percent of the devotees reported that their feelings of dissatisfaction with the group were initiated by restraints that had been placed on the conduct of their social lives within the movement. Those aspects of group affiliation which became most objectionable focused on the regulation of intimate relationships (73%) and regimentation of lifestyle (35%).

TABLE 2
Sources of Social Disillusionment among Disaffected Devotees
(Challenges to Authority)

	% Reporting Conflict over Social Life	*% Reporting Conflict over Spiritual Life*	*% Reporting Conflict over Status Position*	*% Reporting Conflict over Prescribed Sex Roles*
	75	50	35	45
N=40	N=30	N=20	N=14	N=18*

*Sex differences are significant in this category: F=14; M=4

Intimate Relationships

Control over the intimate relationships within the groups, the largest category of dissatisfaction, took a number of different forms including demands for celibacy and the regulation of sexual relations among married and nonmarried couples. Four married couples, two who were affiliated with the Hare Krishna sect and two who were premies in Divine Light Mission, reported that they began to feel resentment and anxiety over the limitations that the religious group placed on their expression of love and intimacy within their marriages. As traditional Hindu-based groups, both of these organizations had laws regarding sexual practices, often limiting sexual relations to one or two times a month. Adherence to such laws was expected of good devotees, and the religious hierarchy admonished those converts who did not follow the laws strictly with regard to their sexual lives. The result was a tension-producing situation for those initiates who had sought and found love through relationships within the community and then felt deprived of that love because of the demands of commitment. As one devotee described this tension:

> Each day there was a certain type of pressure to feel pure. Just a certain type of pressure we would feel that we could never quite do our best. Never be the perfect devotee because we were married. And we were supposed to somehow give up any type of desire for anything in the world that had to

do with the world. . . . . It just got to the point where the thing that was supposed to be an infinite experience was becoming extremely narrow and the love that it was based on was disappearing but not from within me. I felt like there were times when I had a clear conscious experience of just something greater than myself. I had the potential to share with everybody else and particularly my husband and somehow I just feel that a part of me could never 100% buy into feeling guilty. You know like why should I feel guilty? God is love. Why does there have to be some kind of restriction or rule in my life that I should separate from my husband or not make love with my husband so that I could devote myself completely. I just couldn't understand. It is very Hindu, to redirect energy away from sex and toward spirituality, but we could never really see that, accept it totally.

Among the unmarried devotees, grievances with the power structure arose over issues of sexual conduct as well as choices of friendships and personal relationships. The religious hierarchy sought to control romantic involvements outside the group and intimate relations established with other devotees. In the first situation, both men and women reported that their break with the movement came as a result of condemnation for maintaining a love relationship with a nondevotee. The type of pressure brought to bear on the devotee is consistent with the kind of controls that families exert over children who choose love relationships outside the ethnic or religious background of their parents. Similarly, a college student in the charismatic Church of Christ described the pressure he was under to sever all outside ties and to conduct his social and dating life under the strict rigors of the church doctrine. For him, the final break presented an agonizing choice:

> In leaving it was pretty much a slow build-up. I was starting to find things I was dissatisfied about. These were time demands and then there are a set of unwritten rules that don't have anything to do with any kind of scripture. And it is forcibly enforced by the group leaders. There are really strict social norms, very strictly regulating the relationships between men and women. Men and women from the church never ate together. They never drove to church together and seldom sat together. You were expected to go out every Saturday night with a girl from the church and you always went with at least two other couples. You were never supposed to go to the movies or anything. You might go to a nice restaurant and then go home and talk with other members in the church.

When you drove your date home you dropped the woman off first and then you went home. If you deviate from that they come down pretty hard and fast on you. They had rules like you were supposed to be home at 10:00 P.M. I never deviated. I wasn't about to. They wouldn't take any nonsense. Another thing was that you were supposed to go out with a different girl every week. All the sisters are special and if you only know one you don't get to know any of the others. That kind of thing. So it was impossible for any kind of relationship to develop. You were never allowed to go and see a sister during the week. The phone was the only way you could get to talk to someone and then her roommate usually intervened to relay all of the messages.

I never really thought about leaving but at the same time I never thought I would be able to stay. It was never something that I planned on. The situation developed to a point where I just couldn't go anymore. I met this girl outside the church and I was seeing her and they didn't like that at all. So I had to see her secretly and that was also kind of a big thing to try and keep going. And also they don't want you to have any friends outside the group. They say they do but they don't. The way they explain it is that if your biggest number one priority is God and you have friends that aren't interested in God, then how can you be friends with them. It is kind of black and white logic there. If you have a friend outside the church and you invite them and they never come back, you are not supposed to maintain the relationship. Really then, I didn't have much choice in leaving. If I was going to continue to see this woman friend I had become involved with, I had to leave.

Experiences like his were not uncommon among the disaffected devotees, many of whom, like those who had married within the group, viewed their conversion at least partially from the standpoint of meeting specific social needs that had not been satisfied before their commitment. As the imposition of rules and regulations interfere with these social goals, however, challenges to the hierarchy emerge, straining relations among group members. Within the religious movements, doubt or non-conformity create a source of tension for other devotees who often condemn and chastise those who question the norms and values of those in power. The following case of a Bahai follower provides an example in which disillusionment with the movement came as a direct result of the social control vested in a small number of group members. The account of his separation is briefly retold here:

With the Bahais, I was attracted to what it could offer spiritually. In a general way I was attracted to what it stood for, to what it wanted to occur in the world. I wanted some answers and I wanted a father kind of image—what you expect to get from God and religion. . . . If you have a connection with a God it is a concept that works for a lot of people. It can help you develop emotionally and spiritually and you can get yourself together. A lot of people don't have that. They don't have anything that helps them get together.

In my case I had to leave, to give up that connection with the Bahais. The way the faith is set down, it is supposed to work beautifully. It could work but it doesn't. It is the people. In the Bahais there is this council system that operates to solve problems and I had difficulty keeping the laws that the Bahai faith set down. You present a problem and it is pretty cut and dry how they deal with it, advising you what to do according to the scriptures. I was having this relationship with this woman, another Bahai in Newport. She was married and her husband had been away for a year. When he got back, we approached the council. They told her and her husband to remarry in the Bahai faith—the council told her to go back to her husband. I was left with nothing. People are in real pain and suffering and they did not have the answers. They only caused more suffering.

I think that they have something very important. I still believe in the faith. It had been some security for me and I probably could have stayed and grown in the faith. It took me about six months to leave, but I just couldn't live the way they wanted me to.

Regimentation of Lifestyle

While restrictions on marriage and intimacy pose one set of social problems within the movements, other regulatory practices create additional sources of strain. In this regard, challenges to the normative structure of the religious community embrace a wide variety of regulations that are imposed in varying degrees throughout the different religious settings. These include objections to prohibitions on dance, music, food, dress, and sexual relations. Nearly 35 percent of the respondents indicated frustration with the rules and the harsh system of regulation which chastised those who could not keep the laws faithfully and to the letter. Although anger was primarily directed at the hierarchy for making difficult and unrealistic demands on the devotees, a certain amount of anger was turned inward as devotees also blamed themselves for a lack of discipline and commitment. As one devotee expressed his dilemma:

> My whole involvement with the group became a lie. I began to lose any regard at all for what I was supposed to be doing. They had laws for everything. You are supposed to make certain motions when you pray. I would say it was ridiculous and I wouldn't do it. I was doing drugs when I got involved and you are not supposed to do that. I was also drinking. I was living my life the way I wanted to and getting from the faith some measure of security so that I could continue my life that way. But it was like a double life. There were two different worlds I traveled in. One was a crazy and insane world and the other was the faith. It was a gradual process. I just realized it was ridiculous to continue my association with the group.

Another follower of Maharaj Ji spoke of her difficulty with the rigors of ashram life:

> After about a year, I missed my old life. I missed thinking that I would ever be a mother. That's the ashram. When you live in the ashram you live by the ashram rules. Basically the houses are male and female. Those living in the ashram do not have sex or drugs, not even coffee. There is no meat or fish. You know you're like a monk, a nun. And if you break the rules, they know. Toward the end it got crazy. We'd find boys in the closets when we came home at night and I would sneak out and gorge myself and get drunk with my brother. But I felt a lot of pressure. I was an ashram coordinator and I couldn't take the pressure. But I couldn't leave either. It took me at least six months to move away.

Overall, the conflicts over the regulation of social life become the first expression of dissatisfaction with the religious movement. These conflicts are often intensified by the demands of spiritual practice and religious adherence which contribute to the restrictions placed on devotees and which increase the mounting tension over the dilemma of autonomy versus group commitment. Thus, 50 percent of the devotees reported that disillusionment with the power structure extended beyond the area of control over social life and into the religious aspects of commitment as well.

Regulation of Spiritual Life

With respect to the spiritual demands of commitment, respondents reported two major areas of dissatisfaction. These were the time commitments required of followers and conflicts which developed over ideological differences in the exercise of religious discipline and the interpretation of scriptures and teachings.

Conflicts over Time Commitment

Thirty-nine percent of the respondents indicated that separation from the religious group became increasingly desirable as the demands of spiritual practice interfered with other aspects of their life, including work, family, and school. Most often devotees would describe these conflicts in terms of the pressures they felt to be "perfect disciples," an ideal established by the religious hierarchy that could only be achieved through a program of total devotion. Such a program involved daily meditation and lectures in the groups based on Eastern spiritual disciplines and daily Bible study and tri-weekly prayer meetings in the charismatic Christian groups. Typically, salvation and spiritual rewards were made contingent upon fulfilling certain levels of religious practice that were administered and controlled by the higher-status devotees. Absence from prayer meetings or meditative practice were noted by the leadership and followers would be chastised for their lack of discipline, devotion to the charismatic leader, and love of God. In Divine Light Mission, for example, the goals of marriage and family were seen as somewhat mutually exclusive to the goals of total devotion. Here, a female devotee describes the conflict this created for her:

> After a while it just got to be so intense that I couldn't handle it. You know the families were breaking up. I felt like my family was breaking up. I couldn't handle it even though I felt like this is what has to happen. I kept talking to the initiator about it because I kept asking him. I said I really want to dedicate my life, I am supposed to. I want to do that but I am married and he just kept saying then you can't be a perfect devotee, you

can't dedicate your life. I felt guilty but I also felt like this marriage was real. I felt like my marriage and my children came from God and I couldn't just give them up.

The anxiety described by this follower was also expressed by other devotees, who increasingly felt as if they had to make a choice between continued religious commitment and commitment to other significant aspects of their lives. The emotional demands of each, as manifested in expenditures of time and energy, fostered a sense of inadequacy among group members. The difficulties posed by the conflicting demands engendered a diverse set of responses including disdain for the bureaucracy and a personal sense of failure. A Buddhist devotee of seven years explains her feelings in this way.

> The problem was the organizational aspect of the group. People in charge of this and that and so on. It was just too bureaucratic. I don't like it when someone says you have to sit so many hours a week, and I want it written down in this little book that I will check every week. I rebel against that type of authority no matter how much sense it makes. When I first joined it wasn't that way. There were no meditation instructors, no one overseeing your practice. As it got bigger there was a hierarchy and groups that were guards and groups that served at court and groups for business and groups for dance. And I never do well in that type of organization. . . . But my reasons for leaving also have to do with my sense of commitment. I really see it as my inability to make that commitment. What I do sort of regret in myself is that I am not very well disciplined. I just can't make that commitment to practice all the time as much as I know that there is nothing like practice. I do sort of wish that I had the ability to make a solid gesture, instead of being so wishy washy about it. Maybe that will happen in another time in my life.

At times the demands of religious practice took the form of threats and severe group pressure on those members who were acting independently of the movement. This seemed to be especially true for charismatic Christian groups such as the Church of Christ which established a large following among university students. As one young woman described it:

> There was Bible study and services. If you don't go to Bible study or a service you get a lot of pressure and since they are everywhere in the dorms,

in the lounges and cafeterias, it is hard to avoid. I began to have migraine headaches. My school work was not getting done. There was no time for anything but church. One night I decided to study instead of going to Bible class. My roommates told me never to let that happen again. As they were talking to me, I tried to leave. Another friend asked me to stay and she said she would do Bible study with me now. I said all right. Then we began to read the Bible together and this girl started yelling at me, telling me I was possessed for wanting to leave. Then a few other church members came into the room with the sister who was the leader of the dorm floor. They told me I would go to hell if I stopped coming to church. And for a week they never let me alone. Finally, I moved out of the dorm room, and suddenly they just stopped talking to me. A week before they had been hugging and kissing me and now they would not sit at a table with me.

Other students reported similar experiences in which the demands of devotion were to take precedence over all other responsibilities. The pressure to give more time and greater loyalty increased as converts were asked to humble themselves completely. Humility was expected in every area of life and particularly in those areas associated with religious interpretation and teaching. As such, devotees also reported disillusionment with the aspects of commitment that focused on questions of spiritual authority and doctrine.

Conflicts over Religious Doctrine and Practice

Fifteen respondents in the study reported that at least a part of their dissatisfaction with the group was a result of the dogmatic way in which the teachings were presented and the practices applied. For some devotees, the religious dogmatism was in fact the most troubling aspect of their commitment. Among these followers were a former Catholic priest and a nun, each of whom had come to a nontraditional movement in the hope of finding a broader perspective than Catholicism had offered. Their cases are presented here as examples of religiously oriented individuals whose conversion to an alternative movement represents a lifelong quest for spiritual knowledge and a total submersion in the religious experience.

A Journey from the Church to the Ashram. Anne had been a nun for four years when she left the convent at the age of twenty-two to pursue her spirituality through other religious and spiritual orientations. Eventually she joined a Sikh community in New Orleans:

> I have a long history with religion, intensely so. There was a point in my life when I was in my early twenties when I left Catholicism. I had grown up a Catholic and I was intensely Catholic and I left that. I had pretty much explored all the different Western religions. I had gone to all the churches trying to find the place that I felt could be spiritually meaningful to me. Then I knew at that point that I wanted something more universal. The Sikhs were the only alternative in New Orleans. The ashram was not very big, just a few people and that was perfect for me. It wasn't overpowering. You didn't have to wear a turban to live in the ashram. The only thing you had to do was the *sadna* [morning meditation]. I could join in things that I thought were meaningful.
>
> The attraction was to have other people that I could be with and talk with spiritually. I needed companionship on the level of the spiritual. Having gone through the convent, there were processes that were important to me, to my spiritual growth. For example, community, companionship with other people who were at least moving in the same direction of spiritual growth and meaning in their lives. These were the things that attracted me. Community and service were the two things I needed to grow spiritually.
>
> I related to the Sikh teachings more than to Catholicism because I felt they were more universal. Sikhism in its teachings has a lot of universal principles. These appealed to me in their purer teachings, what I consider the spontaneous truths. But as they get established into a group, somehow there is something in the human condition that makes for nonuniversality. I think that happened in Christianity and Sikhism also, although I would never say that or share that with anyone in the ashram. That would be total heresy. Even though the universality is talked about, there is an isolated group that sees themselves as having a mission, a specialness that nobody else has, which is part of the dogma I reject in Christianity and with the Sikhs.
>
> In New Orleans the authority structure was not so much of an issue because they were not as orthodox. But when I moved to California I got into an ashram with eleven or twelve Sikhs and this is the best way I can describe the authority I cannot accept. If we were discussing a topic, something in the news and I would have an opinion and I would say, you know I read in this book, such and such. The answer would be, "You know in the teacher's lecture on this date, he said so and so . . . We will not investigate this issue, because we already know the answer." The teacher is the absolute authority and all of the followers must accept his teachings without question. I just couldn't do that. Having gone through Catholicism and

having vomited this out of me, there was no way I could take it again, under a new content but the same process.

It wasn't the spiritual principles or guidelines. That was what I got that was beautiful and I always took it in. When the teacher or anyone else spoke about anything spiritual I was always open and incorporated a lot of the principles. It was the obedience to a certain set of beliefs and practices that I could not accept. It was the attitude that you had to be at every *sadna* at three in the morning or you were considered a weak devotee. There was no flexibility, only strict adherence to the teacher and to the spiritual regulations of the ashram. I couldn't buy into it. Although I never expressed this openly to anyone, not even to the director when I left. I didn't feel free at all to state that was why I left, because of the demands of overwhelming love and obedience to the teacher.

There were things about the Sikhs I loved, that fulfilled a lot of emotional and personal needs as well as spiritual needs. But there was that one thing that was an absolute—a total resistance in my being to that kind of authority. I just don't think that is the essence of spirituality. And perhaps the teacher himself would agree because in India it is not like that, there is more openness.

A significant point for Anne in her own understanding of the process of spiritual disillusionment is the imposition of social interpretation on the basic teachings of any religious doctrine—the ways in which ideas and principles are shaped by human influence and motivation in the evolution of religion from a body of thought to a social community of followers. Interestingly enough, Daniel, a former priest, spoke to this same dilemma, suggesting that it is not theology itself which is the problem but the interpretation and imposition of religious ideology by those in power who ultimately destroy the spiritual nature of religious movements.

Daniel had been a Roman Catholic priest for thirty years before leaving the church and joining an Eastern-based group in California who were followers of Yogi Nanda. He had spent much of his life in missionary work in Africa and India. While in India, Daniel began to feel that he was learning more from those he was trying to convert than they were learning from him. He was very attracted to the Indian way of life and the religious philosophy of Hinduism. Thus, at the age of sixty, he made the decision to leave the priesthood in order to expand and broaden his religious perceptions. He left India and moved to California where he started a soup kitchen in Los Angeles, married, and then joined the Sunburst religious community where he and his wife were placed in charge of landscaping for the communal farm. Hindu in orientation, Sunburst offered Daniel a daily meditation program the objective of which was to find and become one with God. He and his wife remained at Sunburst for two and a half years. Their decision to leave the group was tied to issues of authority, control, and religious interpretation:

> While we were at Sunburst, we found this book that was part of a foundation in Chicago. There were a group of people who were committed to preserving this book intact. The book is a message for mankind, revelations. At Sunburst, my wife and I began reading this book every day. I went through it in about three months. We were really committed and excited about the book and we were trying to share it with others in the Sunburst community. The founder of the community had seen the book and had read a little of it. He knew that some of the teachings were different than what he was teaching.
>
> A group of older members came to us and told us that it would be better if we remained loyal to their leader, that as long as we were at Sunburst, we should stay with the teachings of the community. That was not the way I could go after all my experience, especially with the dogma of the church. No leader, no matter who he might be, can claim my complete allegiance. God must come first and his voice within me must always take priority. I respected the leader in many ways but I could not accept that what he said was gospel truth. I had to respect my own convictions as well. Through religious history when a religion or teachings are ascribed to a certain person that person is deified and the significance of the religion is lost in the respect or attachment to that individual. I have seen that happen and to me it doesn't matter who is the founder or the medium for the revelation. What is important to me is that it speaks to my heart and to my spirit. At Sunburst, others would not meet with us and read the book. They had been advised otherwise and so we felt an absence of fellowship in the spirit.

The pressure to accept and to conform to only one religious doctrine was somewhat subtle in the experiences of Anne and Daniel. There were no threats or explicit accusations of heresy or damnation, yet the authority structure made it quite clear that challenges, questions, and ideological deviations would not be tolerated. In the charismatic Christian groups, this lack of toleration was expressed through far less subtle means as evidenced by this account from a member of the Church of Christ:

> When I first joined the soul talks, a number of times I found the guys saying something that just wasn't right. I have a strong religious background and they were not always concerned with rightly dividing the Word. One of their biggest aims is to give the impression of a unified front and if a leader says something that is not quite correct, the others just let it slide. No one would say anything. Everyone would smile and nod and there was just kind of this heavy silence. If you challenge the leader, you find out why everyone else is so quiet.
>
> There are eight guys in your soul-talk group and if you express an opinion contrary to their views, they will challenge you on it and it won't go any further than that. If you do it again then you will talk with your soul-talk leader and then after that some of the other soul-talk leaders will talk to you and then some of the other guys from other soul talks come and knock on your door to "encourage" you, which is one of the most ominous experiences you can imagine. Here are all these guys, maybe ten of them, knocking on your door to encourage you. They never actually threaten you physically but they have ways of explaining the situation that you can almost smell the sulfur, threatening you with eternal damnation and hell.

In all three cases presented here, the devotees who challenged the religious ideology were converts who had former religious backgrounds, each having been trained and brought up in strict religious disciplines. Anne and Daniel had a prior commitment to Catholicism in common, while the charismatic church follower had attended Lutheran schools and then a fundamentalist academy before coming to the university and joining the Church of Christ. Other researchers, including Lofland and Stark (1964), have also found that religious converts often have a spiritual orientation to life which can be traced to strong childhood affiliations. Thus, while it is not true for all of the followers of this study, for nearly 40 percent of the respondents, conversion to an alternative movement represented a continuity in the life choices of the individuals rather than a break or deviation from early socialization patterns.

Further, having prior knowledge of and familiarity with both religious doctrine and institutional authority, converts seem to be attracted to as well as repelled by spiritual traditions that are all-encompassing and doctrinaire in their approach. As issues of control infringe on freedom of thought and autonomy of spirit, resistance to the current religious authority is intensified by associations with past affiliations which were characterized by a rigid power structure. In part, this resistance stems from status conflicts in which a devotee, such as Daniel, comes to a new religious group with a prior status in religious matters and authority. As this prior status is unrecognized or acknowledged within the new affiliation, challenges from the devotee are treated as the dissension of any new member or lay disciple.

Problems of status differentiation were not only evident in areas of spiritual expertise and knowledge, but in the power relations that infiltrated all aspects of life within the religious community. For eight devotees in particular, the power struggles in which they became engaged spoke to the nature of sibling-like rivalry that infused the groups with competitiveness and jealousy. For the most part, conflicts over power relations were primarily relevant for male devotees in that gender was often the basis on which high status was either allocated or denied within the movements.

The Politics of Spirituality: Conflicts over Status Positions

The experiences of the male devotees reflect the competitive nature of the patriarchal religious system in which men compete with one another for a limited number of power positions within the community. The result of such competition is the creation of a reward system that offers the promise of social power if one were to achieve leadership status. So compelling is this desire for social power that one male devotee reported withstanding both psychological and physical abuse because his teacher was "grooming" him for leadership. Other respondents were also motivated by the possibility of becoming an elevated disciple or close subordinate of the charismatic leader. As such goals were thwarted, however, devotees would turn their anger toward their peers who were being promoted and selected in place of them. A former Buddhist describes his disillusionment in this way:

> There are people in the administrative hierarchy who are now considered higher than you. And when you have lived with them and you know them it is hard to regard them as someone who can show you anything. And yet they have been singled out. You realize they have been singled out for their administrative abilities and you can't learn anything from them. The structure became difficult to justify, privileged class and aristocracy. They didn't seem to deserve it. A lot of people have lived with this disenchantment.

In addition to vying for promotion and advancement, maintaining a position that has already been established is another source of status conflict that affects male devotees, particularly when the structure of the community changes and becomes more stratified as the movement grows. A good example of this form of politicalization can be found in the experience of a Hare Krishna disciple who remained in the movement for eleven years. As a novice, John joined the sect in New York City when the movement was new to the United States. A drop-out from college, he had been interested in Hatha Yoga and the Hare Krishna approach seemed compatible with the Yoga tradition. He had read about the group in a 1966 issue of *Evergreen Review*, a somewhat radical publication that was being published at the time. That year he attended a Hare Krishna celebration in New York and then went to Montreal where a new temple had just been started. John met the Swami, the founder of the sect, in Montreal, and he developed a personal relationship with him. For a brief time he saw the Swami every day and was given permission to sit in on all his discussions with other disciples.

From the beginning of his involvement, John was more concerned with the theory than with the practice of the religious philosophy. Nonetheless, he spent the first three years in the movement moving from place to place establishing temples in Boston, West Virginia, and Columbus, Ohio. It was not until 1969 that he was able to pursue his interest in theology by setting up a press to translate the Swami's books. By 1971 John had become editor and translator for all the Swami's works and he had taken courses in Sanskrit to become fluent in the language of the scriptures and of the spiritual master. John stayed with the press until 1973 when the Swami returned to India, taking all of his major disciples with him. John, however, was advised to remain in the States with his wife and young son.

After the Swami left, John went to Dallas to start a new temple. He became very depressed and a number of disciples wrote to the Swami about John's condition. A month later the Swami wrote back and invited John to India to take a position as his secretary. John left his family in New York and remained in India with the Swami for the next four years, traveling twice around the world in his capacity as companion and translator to the spiritual master. In the following passage, he tells of his life with the Swami and the changes that took place upon the death of the spiritual leader in 1977:

> The Swami had a personal secretary who was responsible for his well being, someone who gave him a massage every day to minimize his muscle strain, who would also cook and take care of his personal things. Then there was a correspondence secretary who took care of the business affairs as well. And then there was the third secretary and that was me. I was in charge of publications. I would translate his work and then edit it by asking questions and preparing for the press. We traveled with him everywhere and the other secretaries changed. It was kind of like a rotation system to allow other disciples to spend time with him. But I stayed with the Swami throughout. My position did not change.
>
> The Swami died in 1977 and I had been with him until that time. At the end he stopped doing the translations and I would do them and he would ask me to read them to him. Finally, he asked me to finish the thirty-volume work he had been working on right before he died.
>
> His death affected me in a number of ways. Personally the loss was tumultuous. For one thing, other people took over once he died. He had a governing body of twenty-four people all over the world. And he had appointed eleven other people to grant initiation. And then there was me to do the translations. And that was about it. I didn't agree with many of the things that were going on. The pressure they put on people to go out and preach and the pressure to accept what they preached. There were many forms of corruption—power politics, money, and even worse, spiritual corruption. I thought it was criminal the way people would be taken in,

given a snatch of the philosophy in an undynamic way and then sent out on the streets to collect.

Among the eleven initiators there was no one person who had been appointed by the Swami to lead when he died. The Swami in fact appointed the eleven because there was no one who could step into his shoes, although tradition would have one leader. Immediately after his death, people went back to the zones they were in charge of and I stayed in India, translating the last book he had been working on. I had been invited to stay at the last place where the Swami lived and it was beautiful there—the birds, the trees, and the work of the Swami. I was living by myself. I lived outside the temple and I was not directly involved in what was going on outside. But I was concerned so I wrote a letter to the chairman of the governing board and several members stopped by to see me, to hear what I had to say. Then the leaders called a meeting just before the festival of 1979.

At this meeting which was held in India, they began by saying if you have any questions the governing board will be glad to address them. I wanted a discussion so I raised a philosophical point about the teachings and no one said anything. They all looked at me. I was definitely the rebel in the crowd. Most of these people were businessmen. They had harsh criticism for other people who were in India, very harsh criticism. There were police at this meeting and I know the board was capable of violence. These were all men who were swamis who had their own organizations and yet they were insecure because they did not understand the philosophy. They were managers and they discredited anyone who had a knowledge base. At his deathbed, the Swami told everyone that if they had any questions they should go to this one swami. But the governing board made it clear they did not want anyone seeing him once the Swami had died.

I left the meeting before it was over. I felt very threatened there. I wasn't sure what I was going to do and then a few older members suggested that I leave India and go to the West to see if things were as bad as I thought. I went to London and stayed for three years. At first I was welcomed, but then I became the black sheep. The head of the London operation was suspicious of me and he made me feel uncomfortable so that I left the ashram and never moved back. I didn't want to stay until I sorted things out for myself. I didn't want to keep associating with the people who I thought did not have the right values. What was most troubling was the application of the philosophy, the material emphasis in the West that overshadowed the spiritual emphasis in the East.

As the account reveals, the death of the Swami had important consequences for the power structure of the organization. Increasingly, the movement experienced a shift in orientation from a small family-style community to a large-scale commercial endeavor. For John this shift cost him his position in the movement and a crisis of faith, as the philosophy of the Swami seemed to die with the spiritual teacher. Others in the movement expressed similar disillusionment with the political aspects of religious commitment. Peter, another 11-year veteran of Krishna Consciousness, spoke of two incidents in particular that had been devastating to his faith. The first occurred just before the Swami's death when the Western governing board was assuming more and more influence in the running of the organization. During this critical juncture in the movement, the person in charge of the powerful New York temple was accused of embezzling money while he sent the "purists" out into the streets to collect funds. According to Peter's account:

> The money that was coming in for religious purposes was being used to buy and sell yachts down in Miami. And then the temple president lost all the money at one point. And so he defaulted on all the loans and equipment that the New York operation had bought to maintain a large printing business in paperback books. I had bought all the equipment and had set it up and now they foreclosed and the whole commercial scheme failed. At the same time the president's relationships with women were disclosed and of course he had taken a vow of celibacy like all other high-level devotees.
>
> A few people did know what he was doing—seeing women and investing money privately—but he had his goon squads and he would have these people beaten up and thrown out of the temple if they talked about his activities. I remember a few beatings and it was always coming down to me that this guy was stealing. But I had some good friends on the goon squads and they beat up this devotee who was in good standing and he went to the Swami directly and that's when the investigation began.
>
> I was shocked when I found out about the New York leader. I was hurt and the whole temple was in a sort of state of shock for six months. The Governing Board sent a delegation, very high pressure. They said this guy had screwed up, that he was a bum, but that we were all righteous and they were sorry but it was a mistake. I didn't think about leaving yet. In fact, I was put in charge of the temple as vice president. They said I needed to put things into shape. I said okay I'll manage the temple for six months and then I want to go to India after this. I said let me go to India and sit down and meditate.

After six months, Peter did go to India where he was made president of the Bengali district and placed in charge of a temple outside of Calcutta. There he supervised the work of hundreds of Bengali refugees who were constructing a new building for the movement. He also contracted a severe case of hepatitis and was hospitalized, at which point other members called his parents and told them that their son was dying and that he needed money to come home. His parents sent him $500 and he returned to the United States to recover. Once he was well, he considered leaving the movement and then the Governing Board asked him to take over as president of the New York temple:

> I was left in charge of this skyscraper. The boilers weren't working, no
> hot water. It was the middle of a New York winter. We were bouncing
> checks all over the place. There was a $12,000 a month mortgage to pay
> and they said, here it is. We are going to India for the festival. It was defi-
> nitely a power trip to have 300 or 400 people under you who you were
> looking after, looking out for, literally governing their life from feeding to
> clothing to shelter.

After three months as the temple President in New York, Peter left and went to Germany, disenchanted with the Governing Board and the "sales pitch" mentality that had taken over the movement. In Germany he worked with Krishna Consciousness in an evangelistic capacity, touring Poland, Czechoslovakia, and Hungary. But in West Germany he found the same pressure to be a salesman rather than a spiritual follower and he returned to the States, this time to California. The final year of his commitment, the Board offered him nothing; there was no presidency and no position in the West Coast community. For the first time he was on his own, without a specified status in the group. He knew many of the temple's leaders in California and he was accorded a certain amount of respect but his own power base had diminished considerably.

At this point in his commitment, Peter's faith had definitely been shaken by the attitude of the Governing Board and his loss of status. As he describes it, in a last act of desperation, he and a friend broke into the archives of the Los Angeles temple. The archives supposedly housed letters the Swami had written on his deathbed, in which he appointed the eleven board members to their positions as leaders of the movement. When they broke into the archives, no letters were found:

> I found they had appointed themselves as gurus. They had conned the whole organization into thinking they had been appointed by the Swami before his death, as if it had been divine intercession. But it was a con. When he was dying, they conspired to get everyone else out of the room and when he died they came out and said he has appointed us, we are now in charge, the absolute authority. They had a few tapes and the tapes were in the archives locked in a vault. We broke into the vault and listened to the tapes. We found that the Swami didn't appoint these guys to be gurus at all. The only thing he said on the tapes was that you can now manage the movement. For me, he didn't say you are now divine or holy.

The betrayal Peter felt at finding the tapes was the final turning point. The board members were simply disciples like himself who had taken over the administrative aspects of the organization. They had no real claim to godliness and thus, for this devotee, their power base was not legitimate.

In an interesting finale to a long and painful association with the Hare Krishnas, Peter used what political leverage he had (his knowledge of the tapes) to "acquire" a wife through an arranged marriage with the Los Angeles temple. "At the time I really wanted to get married," he said. "The president knew I had snuck in and gotten this information so he said, 'I'll give you the disciple you want if you'll shut up about the tapes.' I agreed and she agreed and we got married and left."

This last case history illustrates the importance of political power relations within these movements and the effects of such relations on devotees who are seeking to fulfill status goals through conversion. Each time Peter was ready to leave, he was offered a different position that would quell his doubts temporarily and appeal to a desire for his own source of power. When he had exhausted all avenues of legitimate status acquisition, having been lured into presidential posts that were grueling and difficult to manage, his disillusionment led to an act of rebellion (breaking into the archives) rather than to immediate separation. Believing that at last he had found the truth about the Swami and his successors, Peter then used his inside knowledge as a bargaining tool to satisfy a growing desire for love and marriage.

Thus, in the politics of spirituality, power and authority can become associated with commercialism and greed, as some disciples are abused and brutalized for their unwillingness to accept the direction of the governing body, while others are rewarded with powerful positions that act to strengthen a failing commitment. In this system of power relations, women are often objectified, as the example of Peter's marriage suggests, by a bartering system in which their only access to power is through relationships to high-status men in the movement. Thus for female devotees, issues of status and reward may be tied to personal relationships involving sexual intimacy and control. Among the respondents who reported such experiences (N=5), sexual relations with the men in power were held out as a reward or privilege for those devotees who would be allowed to know God's love in this way. As such, some of the women expressed a willingness and desire to engage in sexual relationships with the spiritual teacher, as the promise of enlightenment might be that much closer if one were to have a physical relationship with a godly being. Further, such intimacy provided one of the few means of social status available to female devotees who were selected to become the consort to the leader or one of his chosen disciples.

Certain groups, particularly those associated with Tantric Buddhism and Hinduism, have sexual meditative practices as part of their religious philosophy and training and it is here where women are most likely to compete for the position of consort, either on a temporary or more permanent basis. The selection process is often controlled by high-status devotees, those men who are the intermediaries between the followers and the charismatic leader. The case of Sheila illustrates the way in which female devotees become disillusioned as a result of sexual rejection and denial.

Sheila joined an Eastern religious movement the summer after her graduation from college. The leadership of the movement was vested in one spiritual master, the Yogi, and a number of his close male disciples who composed the administrative hierarchy. These "elevated" disciples were the teachers or gurus empowered with authority from the divine master. Early in her involvement, Sheila established affective ties to one guru who came to dominate her life within the movement. It was he who controlled access to the spiritual master and repeatedly advised her never to enter into a sexual relationship with the Yogi, although such a relationship was common among the other female members. After seven years in the movement, she described her bitter disillusionment in this manner:

> It was the screwing system of the great harem. Because my guru told me never to sleep with the Yogi, I never had sex with him so I was never promoted. And when he came to America he never talked to me, never loved me. He only loved those who screwed him. It didn't matter what I thought because I wasn't screwing the Yogi. Spiritual energy and sexual energy are the same thing in America. They took everything away and ignored the heart.
>
> The daggers of sexuality were drawn to make one person feel very bad and one person feel very good. The aggressiveness was competitive. Sex was also used as a punishment. If someone was negative they were put down sexually. Sex was a way to pull people.

Sheila eventually left the movement broken both spiritually and emotionally. For her and for the other women involved in similar situations, the sexual dynamic of religious commitment posed problems of creating a spiritual identification that was strongly tied to sexual intimacy with the men in power, an intimacy which was also tied to romantic illusions of love and commitment. In effect, the hierarchy maintained control over who would be the recipient of such love and as such, anger and resentment were often directed at the guru's subordinates rather than at the leader himself who remained, at least for a period of time, a loving figure in the perception of the female devotees.

The system of competitiveness that develops through the sexualization of religious commitment contributes to the erosion of bonds among female devotees as the need and desire for male approval become the focus for status and self-esteem in the male dominant culture. One young woman articulated this aspect of her love for the guru very clearly:

> He kept the other women in line. For the first time I could be myself wholly without women being jealous of me. I was told I was being protected and I was feeling protected. That's where the love began.

The effect of the patriarchal system of authority is that the breaking of social bonds proceeds along gender lines. Men vie for positions of power within the hierarchy while women are placed in subordinate roles wherein they compete for the attention and approval of the more powerful males. Under both conditions, the bonds of sisterly and brotherly love are strained by the competitive environment of the religious community. It is significant to note, however, that the sexual aspects of commitment affect male devotees as well; many experience jealousy over the intimacy permitted the women with respect to their alliances with the charismatic leader. One group solved this problem by creating a guard system that permitted men to remain physically close to the founder throughout his daily activities. In another movement male homosexuality offered the possibility of physical intimacy with the leader. In this community it was primarily young boys who were chosen for this relationship.

The sexual division of responsibility evident in functions such as female consort and male bodyguard illustrates the nature of sex roles within the religious communities. While not all of the movements had such stringent forms of sex-typing, restrictive sex roles were often cited as a major cause for disillusionment with the religious group. Existing research on sex roles and religious commitment has found that women in alternative movements are for the most part restricted to traditional female roles (Culpepper, 1978; Wallis, 1978; Jacobs, 1984). Such restrictions can lead to departure from the group as they are perceived to be obstacles to fulfilling the social and spiritual goals of affiliation.

Prescribed Sex Roles

Forty-five percent of the followers in this study reported that restrictive sex roles contributed significantly to their dissatisfaction with the religious movement and with the power structure that allocated responsibility and status according to gender. As one might expect, the majority of devotees (78%) who expressed disillusionment with the sexual hierarchy were women. Among those who opposed the sexism in the groups, half of the female devotees reported that they were unaware of sex-role limitations when they first joined the movement, while the other half indicated that they had been attracted to the ideology of clear-cut role separations but became progressively disenchanted when the assumption of the female role led to demands for subservience and submission. In becoming aware of the consequences of sexism within the groups, the women either challenged the authority structure unsuccessfully or left without a confrontation. In either case, a sense of futility pervaded the devotees who recognized that the attitudes toward women originated with religious ideologies which were deeply ingrained in the structure of the movements.

Domestic service and fund raising were the two most common responsibilities associated with female membership. Virtually all of the women in the study reported some aspect of domestic work that was considered part of their role within the group and was distinguished from the spiritual duties assigned to men. For example, the women in Divine Light Mission, the Hare Krishna sect, and the Sikh movement, all Hindu-based groups, were assigned roles as housemothers and housekeepers within the ashram organization. As housemothers, they had primary responsibility for cooking, cleaning, and child care while the men attended to teaching and leadership duties within the spiritual communities. Similarly, within the charismatic Christian movements, the traditional subordinate role for women was emphasized. Women were expected to treat their husbands' authority with the respect accorded God and to function as wives and mothers within the specific Christian tradition that defined female spirituality within the context of domestic values. In addition, direct service to the church was also carried out through the domestic role. One former devotee described the nature of her responsibilities within the church:

> I approached the pastor because I felt I had grown to a point where I could be of use to teach. I was not allowed to do so and the reason I was given was that I'm a woman. I was given a position of authority. I was made a deaconess. A deaconess does the dishes and waxes the floor.

Titles like deaconess or housemother were often bestowed on the women with the expectation that they would fulfill the responsibilities of the organization that were defined as female, a definition that was predicated on the traditional patriarchal view that women could best serve the religious order by serving the men that were closest to God. A Hare Krishna follower explained the perspective in this way:

> The philosophy was that women could not be seen or heard. They agitate men if they are around. . . . After a while I began to do for my teacher what you do for a husband. I would clean things and put flowers in his room. For me it was a pure thing just to be near him, to listen to him speak.

Domestic service was perhaps the most prevalent sex role function associated with religious service. In some cases this aspect of female commitment was intensified by the additional responsibilities of recruitment of new members and the solicitation of funds, both of which became tied to the specific attributes of female spirituality.

According to David Bromley and Anson Shupe (1980), the financial viability of many of the alternative religious movements is dependent on the individual fund-raising activities of the devotees. Thus it is essential that fund-raising and recruitment be aligned with the specific role definitions of the group members. In the case of the female devotees, spiritual growth was often measured in terms of the ability to collect money, as one devotee reported:

> The philosophy was the more books you sell, the more spiritual you are. . . . The best way to serve was to make money. The most perfect thing to do was to go out and sell books. They told us to use our female tendencies to get people to contribute and therefore to purify them and ourselves. At my best, I was bringing in $400 a day. I became very good at it. But when I couldn't collect money any more, I lost my value to the community.

A similar strategy has been discussed by Roy Wallis (1978) in his study of the Children of God. In this analysis he describes "Flirty Fishing," a practice of solicitation and recruitment developed among female members.

> Between 1973 and 1975, a new form of proselytizing activity was beginning to be developed by the Children of God. At first it was experimented with only by the movement's leader and a chosen group of associates, and references to it were at first rather oblique in the Family's literature.

Progressively, more was revealed, until in 1975 a lengthy series of "Mo Letters" discussed this development in explicit detail. The ministry was known as "flirty fishing," and in short it involved the utilization of the sexual attractiveness of young female members as a means of recruiting new disciples and allies for the Children of God. (p. 72)

The effect of this focus on female sexuality is to create a situation in which the women come to assess their spiritual value in terms of their ability to raise money, a skill which they often correlate with their ability to be sexually enticing. This becomes particularly problematic in those movements such as the Hare Krishna and the Unification Church where women are expected to be chaste, virtuous, and pious, three attributes that are in direct conflict with their role as procurer for the religious community. The contradiction in role definition often leads to confusion and loss of self-esteem as the devotee is told to be virtuous and domestic within the group, and to be sexual and seductive outside of the group in order to recruit new members and attract donations.

The greater the emphasis on sexuality in this context, the greater the tendency among the devotees to equate spiritual goals with sexual identity and to associate a failure to meet these goals with a failure as a woman. Because proselytizing is described within the scope of spiritual responsibilities, it takes the place of ritualistic participation which is defined as the male domain. The overall effect of performing traditional sex roles within a rigid male authority structure creates a system within which men are dominant, women are submissive, and the exercise of male power leads to the almost total subordination of female devotees. Challenges to that subordination appear to come at critical times, when the devotee is told in no uncertain terms what her value is as a female and why this should be so according to scriptural references to her inferiority. In discussing the reasons his wife ultimately left the Hare Krishna sect, one man referred to the way she had been treated throughout her years of commitment:

It is horrible the way women are treated. The perspective is that husbands lead and the wife goes along and does what he tells her to do and this is justified by his position. You have to understand this in the context of the religious orientation. I acted with that authority and she accepted it in theory, but in practice there were always problems.

The really bad treatment was in the subtle ways women were made to feel incompetent and inferior. A woman would do something and a man would come along and do it over. Over the years it would mount up, women losing their self-esteem, feeling like they can't do anything right for themselves. And there was this constant bombardment with lectures and it is in the books, women are a lesser being. That is what they learn.

In the most extreme cases the lessons in obedience and subservience are carried into the realm of domestic violence. One such case, that of a young Christian woman, is representative of the accounts told by other abused women, particularly those associated with charismatic Christian groups. Cheryl was twenty years old when she joined a Christian movement that had a missionary organization in Central America. She and her fiancé worked as health-care providers in Bolivia and then returned to the United States where they were both baptized as Christians and then married in their new faith. Within weeks of their marriage, Cheryl's husband began to have violent outbursts during which he would criticize her for the time she spent on her studies at school, time he felt should be devoted to caring for him and for the household.

In this period of their early marriage, they were attending church regularly as well as participating in mandatory Bible studies. Cheryl took the scriptures very seriously and she tried to live by the guidelines the Bible established for Christian wives. But she also had career goals. She wanted to teach and she attended the university as well. Her young husband, also a student, appeared to support her goals when she first returned to school and yet his anger increased over the months. Increasingly, he became physically abusive.

Throughout the two years of her ordeal, Cheryl remained a faithful Christian, seeking help from the church elders who had forbidden her to participate in any outside counseling. Instead they quoted to her from the scriptures, reminding her that the submissive wife is the woman who is in God's favor. Repeatedly, they told her that if she created a good Christian home and was an obedient wife, her husband would have no reason to be abusive. She listened to them and tried to become more pious, but the beatings only grew worse and more frequent. After one particularly violent incident, she went to see the church elders once more and this time she asked if they would approve of her leaving her home for a little while. They advised her to stay, to take the beatings and submit to her husband's authority under any circumstances. After that incident, Cheryl experienced what she described as a crisis in faith. Staying with the church, adhering to their interpretation of the scriptures, meant placing herself in real danger, perhaps even death, and she could not accept that definition of God's love.

The first step Cheryl took, a change that other abused wives in religious movements also made, was to stop attending church. The second was to seek outside counseling, and the third was to separate from her abusive husband, a separation that was made more difficult by the fear that she was now doomed by God and in danger of retribution from her vengeful spouse. After the separation, her husband called her constantly and quoted from the Bible, warning her that divorce was sinful and that she had become a sinner herself. The day of the divorce proceedings, Cheryl recalled that he brought a small book with him from which he began to read aloud on the wickedness of feminism among good Christian women.

What is of interest in this aspect of disaffection is the feminist consciousness that seems to develop among the female devotees who begin to perceive their issues with authority quite clearly in terms of the male-dominated religious structure. Two examples illustrate the ways in which rejection of the hierarchy also comes to mean a rejection of male power and dominance. The first example is that of a follower of Hinduism whose commitment began to wane after a series of interactions with a number of high-level disciples who had made her feel ashamed and humiliated. In this excerpt from her interview, she describes her feelings about her experience:

> What is self-realization? Making people into doormats forever? That is religion? That is *dharma*? That is how you treat women? They talk nonstop for days and days to make someone feel bad, to make someone feel inferior so they can dominate them. They are not taking anyone to God. They're just promoting themselves.

The second statement comes from the former charismatic Christian who left the movement when she was denied a teaching position. She evaluated her experience with the church in very explicit feminist terms:

> When the pastor told me I couldn't teach because I was a woman, I proceeded to get on my high horse. I'm not going to take this kind of stuff. The scriptures say one thing and they act in a totally different way. I tend to be a feminist and I simply could not take this sort of thing.

Conflicts over prescribed sex roles are thus experienced by female devotees at a number of different levels and in various degrees of dissatisfaction. What appears to be most fundamental about this source of disillusionment is the underlying value system of the religious groups which foster notions of female inferiority and male dominance. These values are expressed through the restrictions placed on female participation and in the more extreme situations, the legitimation of violence against women. The result for many of the female followers is the choice between continued submissiveness and a diminished self-image, or separation and a re-evaluation of spiritual goals as these are defined and achieved through a male authority structure. The impact of gender on spirituality and particularly the relationship with the charismatic God figure will be further explored in chapter 4.

Vacillation and the Process of Social Separation

As the analysis thus far suggests, social defection from religious movements involves an interweaving of social and political dissatisfaction which culminates in a move toward physical distancing and separation from the group. Often the first step in making the break is to visibly leave the community. At the time of disillusionment with the social aspects of commitment, 73 percent of the respondents were living within the confines of the religious group. These living arrangements included communes, ashrams, temples, and church facilities. Moving out of the community thus became a means for establishing independence from the movement. However, more than half of the followers (63%) returned at least once to the religious community before making the final break. In a typical case, the devotee would become dissatisfied to the point of leaving but would then find that living apart posed problems of loneliness, isolation, and ambivalence about desertion of the faith. Many returned to the movement in an effort to reestablish bonds with the religious community. The tendency toward vacillation is evident in the experience of Robert who had been raised in a middle-class Jewish family before traveling East to Nepal where he joined a monastic Buddhist sect. Here he describes his commitment and the changes that took place for him:

The monastery was in the forest. We were celibate and we were ascetics. We begged for food from the village and we made a contract to stay five years. As the five years came up, I thought about what it would be like to leave, to pursue a spiritual path without denial and excluding the sensory pleasures.

Leaving meant taking off the robes, entering back into the world outside the monastery. But I wasn't scared. Before when I thought about it, it was terrifying. But as the time came closer, as my contract was up, I began to look forward to it. And the guru told me I would be able to take care of myself now. The depression I had known was gone. When I left I went back to the States where there were other Buddhists. I worked on a farm and I practiced Zen Buddhism. It was not the same as the sect in Nepal but my studies and associations followed a progression.

I began to develop relationships with women and with others who were also on the path. But after a year or so I went back to Nepal. I felt more at home there than I had been in the States. But this time it was different. There were too many distractions. I could not reenter the monastic life as before, the connection was not there. I stayed for nine months and then returned to the States again.

For a smaller number of followers, those who had not participated in communal living as part of their commitment, leaving the movement meant ceasing to attend services, prayer meetings, and meditation sessions. As one angry devotee expressed her decision to stop attending a charismatic church: "It just got so that I couldn't go any more. It really felt good leaving the church. It was almost like the ultimate 'fuck you'."

In leaving religious movements the physical act of separation is the first step toward the creation of a separate identity. Moving out of the ashram or ceasing to attend prayer meetings, like leaving home, is a gesture of independence which provides the psychological distance necessary to reassess the experience of commitment apart from the daily interaction with other group members. Yet such departures often signify states of partial deconversion, as ties to the charismatic leader remain strong even as loss of faith in the community of followers intensifies.

Throughout the accounts of religious conversion, devotees would speak of the abuse, pain, and anguish they had suffered and yet these painful emotional experiences would be attributed to the corruption of the hierarchy or the mismanagement of the bureaucracy. It was not uncommon for a follower to report that he or she believed that the leader did not really know what was going on, or that in his holiness, the charismatic founder must have a plan in the abuse of his subjects. The willingness and the desire to exonerate the leader was perhaps the most consistent theme that appeared throughout the accounts of conversion and disaffection. Long after many of the devotees had moved out of the temples and the ashrams, long after they were no longer attending church, the connection to the God figure remained paramount in their consciousness.

4.

The Leader-Follower Relationship

Charisma and the Unconscious

As the earlier chapters have suggested, the strength of commitment to the charismatic leader is expressed through affective ties that closely parallel the bonds between parent and child. These bonds, unlike the social ties to the community, are formed at deeper levels of the unconscious and therefore have a greater impact on the individual than the adoption of the social identity associated with group affiliation. The charismatic authority attributed to the leader derives from a process of internalization through which the leader is identified with three representations in the unconscious: the symbol of the divine; the idealized parent image; and the idealized self. Each of these unconscious associations contribute to a form of contemporary idolatry wherein the charismatic leader is both loved and revered by his followers. As love becomes the defining emotion experienced during conversion, the notions of surrender and submission become dominant themes in the charismatic relationship.

The Surrender to the Divine Father

In every group studied here, the religious leader was identified with the divine aspects of existence, the transcendental quality of charisma to which Weber referred when he explained the apparent authority and obedience attributed to a charismatic ruler. According to Weber, charisma stems from "devotion to the extraordinary and unheard of, to what is strange to all rule and tradition and which therefore is viewed as divine. It is devotion born of distress and enthusiasm" (Gerth & Mills, 1946:249). In the charismatic religious groups, the connection to the divine is an especially powerful source of bonding in that the leader has both a symbolic value in his direct link to God and a physical manifestation in the ongoing interpersonal dynamic that exists between follower and spiritual mentor. As such, the unconscious process of merging is heightened by the personalized nature of religious commitment.

Among the religious devotees, the leaders were either considered deities themselves, like Guru Maharaj Ji, or were assumed to have godlike qualities which brought them closer to an understanding of reality beyond the material world of everyday life. As one Tibetan Buddhist devotee expressed this feeling, "I suppose I thought Rinpoche was like God, something more than human because he had powers that were supposedly godly. And he could always accomplish anything he wanted to accomplish." Others expressed similar sentiments such as "Maharaj Ji is the Lord to be on this planet" or "the pastor had a direct connection with God and as his emissary spoke for God on earth."

In order to understand the significance of the divine and transcendent attributes of charisma, it is necessary to consider once again the world of total meaning that religious affiliation offers. From a functional perspective, this affiliation provides a structure to one's life which is manifested not only in rules and regulations but in a theology that gives meaning to the concepts of salvation, immortality, and the nature of human experience. As the leader comes to represent the attainment of this spiritual ideal, he is endowed with a quality of otherworldliness which is desired by the religious disciple. Thus conversion contains the elements of a spiritual quest that has as its goal the resolution of ultimate life issues through a connection to the divine in the person of the charismatic leader.

Placing the notion of a spiritual quest in a psychological framework, Underhill (1955) maintains that the search for spiritual knowledge involves an understanding of the unconscious mind which is revealed through religious devotion and practice. The spiritual endeavor is then described as one in which the individual seeks unification with some greater Being, call it God or the transcendental reality. Wilber (1980) speaks of this aspect of human consciousness as a search for the "perennial philosophy":

> . . . or wu, or satori. This is what Plato meant by stepping out of the cave of shadows and finding the Light of Being; or Einstein "escaping from the delusion of separateness." This is the aim of Buddhist meditation, Hindu Yoga, and of Christian mystical contemplation. That is very straightforward; there is nothing spooky, occult, or strange in any of this—and this is the perennial philosophy. (1980:6)

In the small religious movements, this wholeness or unification, the successful discovery of the perennial connection, is tied to the relationship with the spiritual teacher, the leader who is the individual and personal manifestation of one who has attained this level of consciousness and offers the means through which others can also become whole. The desire for wholeness is revealed through deep feelings of love for the charismatic leader which are evident in a consciousness of subservience adopted by the religious devotees. The mentality of subordination that develops among followers is tied to ideals of surrender and sacrifice that are associated with becoming a true disciple. As a devotee of Buddhism described these feelings: "At one time I really wanted to give up my life for my teacher. I really loved him and I had this romantic kind of thing that I would be forced to give up everything to serve him."

Similar feelings were expressed by other followers who perceived their spirituality in terms of submission, obedience, and subservience. Here a female disciple of Circle of Friends describes her first encounter with a man who she believed would become her guru and spiritual advisor:

> He was on the beach playing his guitar and talking about this religious group he had founded, a group he wanted to take to India. He was dressed in soft clothes and he began to play his music. I was really tuned in to his soul. His singing was coming out like divine energy and I thought, I really love this man. I felt like I loved this person so much. I thought, how may I serve you? How may I learn from you? Here was something I really wanted

to get in touch with, that part of him that was so spiritual. Right then I realized I wanted to go to India and be with him.

The formation of affective bonds thus begins with a devotional love that joins the follower to the leader in a relationship of service and obedience. At this stage of the merging process, the symbolic representation of God is primarily expressed in paternal imagery which incorporates associations of deep affection and authority within the unconscious of the religious devotee. The emotional character of charismatic relationships is thus suggestive of the follower's identification with a father figure who is internalized as both a symbol of love and power within the context of the religious family. Further, the leader is endowed with a quality of omnipotence through which he is perceived to know all thoughts and actions of his followers. The following quote describes the sense of vulnerability that is engendered by the godly father figure:

> You would love to spend all day every week with Rinpoche. He is a tremendous man. Everything he does is so enlightening and to just be around him that is a tremendous process. It could just be great, but on the other hand it could also be excruciating. He is the kind of person that just lays you bare. There is no putting up a false front with him. He knows who you are and so in that respect it could be pretty scary. You've got to be willing to bare yourself to that.

The most intense example of this type of internalization was expressed by a devotee who had been raped while a member of an Eastern group. In describing the assault, she spoke of her awareness of the inner voice of her spiritual teacher:

> I followed the inner god. I followed the voice of my spiritual teacher and I failed. I had to follow the voice of my spiritual teacher because he had some plan for me. It was just a test to see if you could be faithful to him no matter what.

For the majority of followers, merging with the leader is experienced as a primary connection to an omnipotent parent on whom the devotee relies for love, protection, and external control. This form of internalization, described in the work of ego psychologists like Freud and Heinz Kohut, is representative of the relationship between the patriarchal father and the powerless dependent child. Other forms of internalization, however, are also evident in the accounts of devotees and suggest that disciples experience different states of merging with the god figure. Within this interpretive framework, the nature of internalization embraces a notion of greater and lesser identification between the follower and the leader as the disciple moves further along a continuum of undifferentiation until there is no distinction between self (devotee) and other (God). Accordingly, the first stage of merging is expressed through the child/parent metaphor, while the second stage involves the projection of an ego ideal onto the leader. The final stage of unification is the experience of mystical union with the charismatic figure. At each level of internalization, the ego boundaries between the leader and follower become increasingly blurred and less distinct.

Charisma and Spiritual Union

The merging of ego boundaries through religious conversion reflects a strong desire on the part of the devotee to achieve the perfection of the charismatic leader. Typically, devotees would express their feelings in this way: "I wanted to be just like him. He was the most perfect human being, the most spiritual." Others said that they saw in the teacher the qualities of knowledge, understanding, and love they wanted for themselves. As one follower commented, "I stayed because I thought if I tried, if I did all of the practice and all of the discipline, I would become like him. I would see what he sees and I would truly know God."

The projection of the ego ideal onto the leader helps to explain the intense feelings of love, devotion, and blind faith that become associated with charismatic bonding. In discussing the relationship between love and the ego ideal, Freud wrote (1960:56):

> It is even obvious, in many forms of love-choice, that the object serves as substitute for some unattained ego ideal of our own. We love it on account

of the perfection which we have striven to reach for our own ego, and which we should now like to procure in this roundabout way as a means of satisfying our narcissism. . . .

Yet as the ego ideal is realized through a total identification with the god figure, the meaning of surrender embraces a spiritual dimension that transcends the confines of worldly love, reframing the unconscious connection to the leader in the context of mystical union with the divine. Fourteen respondents reported merging experiences in the tradition of mystical revelations that were described in one of three ways: the experience of bliss, the sensation of an all-encompassing love and warmth, and the merging of ego identities between follower and leader. The first and most frequent form of merging is revealed through the accounts of blissful experiences such as those described by the followers of Maharaj Ji. In these accounts devotees express states of joy, happiness, and transcendence as they merge with the young guru in rituals of enlightenment:

> With Maharaj Ji there was the kind of beyond-the-mind direct experience. It is an incredibly powerful spiritual experience that happens at the festivals. You come before your guru and it's like you just sit there and bliss out. It is very intense and you can feel a part of his cosmic consciousness and you want that feeling all of the time.

Other experiences of merging are expressed as sensations of unconditional love which emerge in the presence of the spiritual teacher:

> One day during meditation a light suddenly shone and I knew that I was consciously experiencing a new reality. The new reality was the personal and unconditional love of my heavenly father. All my life I had indeed addressed God as father but never had I experienced such an intimate, trusting, and joyous father-son relationship as I did now.

The final form of merging reported by the respondents suggest a transformation of consciousness in which the ego boundaries between leader and follower have been totally dissolved. This fusion of self and other is most commonly found among disciples of Eastern-based movements whose religious practices attempt to break down the ego and eliminate the "illusion of separateness." Here a Hindu disciple describes the revelation of wholeness:

> Through the words of the guru, I could feel myself expanding, my spirit lifting and my physical being becoming irrelevant. I became part of everything around me. I realized that separateness did not exist.

Of the fourteen accounts of mystical union, only two such experiences were reported by female devotees. The gender differences in religious experience that are apparent at the social level of commitment are therefore also evident in the affective domain of charismatic bonding. The phenomena of merging and the internalization of the charismatic leader as both a paternalistic god figure and a masculine ego ideal raise significant questions concerning the meaning of paternal bonding in the unconscious and the parallel predominance of the patriarchal deity in the realm of the divine.

The Significance of Gender in Charismatic Bonding

Because of the paternal orientation of charismatic bonding in religious movements, the psychoanalytic approach to religious experience offers insight into the nature of conversion and the meaning of spiritual union. In particular, object relations theory has been used to explain the internalization of God and the desire for union with a deified being. In this interpretive framework, the phenomenon of merging is cast in a regressive context in which the symbiotic union with the god figure is understood as the "need for the sustained, external existence of an immutably protective, loving object" (Ross, 1975) in the manner of the mother-child relationship. The bliss and joy of religious experience thus represents the nondifferentiated state of equilibrium characteristic of infancy and early childhood. As such, conceptions of heaven, paradise, and immortality involve fantasies of wholeness, projected onto God, which reflect the initial state of maternal union (Pollock, 1975).

An apparent contradiction in the object relations model of religious phenomena is the role that gender assumes in the process of unconscious transference. God and the charismatic leader as the personification of God are clearly masculine figures who define transcendence within a patriarchal framework. Symbiosis, however, as the driving motivation in the unconscious, is perceived as a desire for reunification with the feminine, the mother figure. In this regard, Lilian Rubin (1983) further elaborates the object relations perspective:

> . . . from the beginning, life is a process of forming attachments, internalizing representations from the external world, and making identifications with significant people from the world. Since it is the mother who is the primary caregiver—who feeds us, shelters us, holds us in her arms to allay our fears—it is she with whom we make our first attachment, she with whom we form a symbiotic bond within which we do not yet know self from other. For each of us then, whether a girl or boy, it is a woman who is in this primary position in our inner life—a woman who is the object of our most profound attachment, a woman who becomes our first loved other.
> . . .

In adopting the psychoanalytic interpretation of spiritual union, an important question to consider is how and why the source of spiritual identification in the unconscious becomes masculine when the object of primary love is feminine. G. H. Pollock solves the gender inconsistency by describing the spiritualized love object as genderless:

> It is my contention that the omnipotent figure is genderless and is the representation of the first omniscient parent—the maternal being. Symbiotic reunion with this maternal, genderless god figure allows entry into the pregenital heaven and paradise. . . . (1975:34)

For Pollock then, God is both without gender and is maternal, an interesting contradiction in terms. Freud (1950), on the other hand, acknowledges only the primacy of the patriarchal father in religion, suggesting that while the mother may be the earliest source of protection in a child's life, she is soon replaced by the father as protector and provider. Thus, he saw a parallel in the relationship between father and child, God and adult.

The elimination of the mother (that is, the female) as a significant source of primal identification in the spiritual realm is of particular significance to this researcher, especially if one considers the social and political ramifications of a religious history which has witnessed over centuries of human thought and development a shift in spiritual identification from "mother consciousness" to "father consciousness" (Lerner, 1986; Wilber, 1981). In a contemporary manifestation of this shift, the male charismatic leader represents the primary love object with which unification is sought. In order to explain the predominance of this masculine spiritual tradition and the way in which this tradition has evolved within the context of the patriarchal family structure characteristic of small religious movements, it is helpful to consider two aspects of Western culture: the devaluation of the feminine in the spiritual realm; and the predominance in industrialized society of a family structure in which men are often only marginally involved in the affective realm of family life. While these two characteristics of Western society may at first seem unrelated to each other and to religious conversion, *per se*, it is possible to view the interrelationship between these two effects of culture for the impact they have on charismatic bonding within the religious group.

The Devaluation of the Feminine in the Spiritual Realm

Over the last decade there has been increasing interest in the area of spirituality with respect to masculine and feminine god concepts and the way in which notions of deity and spiritual consciousness have in Western thought been defined primarily in male terms through a clearly anthropomorphic representation of a masculine god figure. Among feminists in particular, research into this phenomenon has resulted in a growing body of religious theory which reevaluates the traditional patriarchal view of history and religious development in Western civilization. Two areas of study are of particular significance: the scholarship which is devoted to the recovery of the feminine in Judeo-Christian tradition; and the investigations into the historical antecedents of patriarchal religion as these are related to the ancient practice of goddess worship. Both areas of research suggest the existence of a female-centered spiritual tradition which was either destroyed or reduced to insignificance in the transition from goddess-worshipping to god-worshipping societies.

With regard to the presence of a female spiritual power in Judeo-Christian tradition, the work of June Singer in *Androgyny* (1976) and Elaine Pagels in *The Gnostic Gospels* (1981) is perhaps the most illuminating. In both of these works, the researchers maintain that in the transition to monotheism and the advent of patriarchal religion in the West, the feminine aspects of a spiritual consciousness were either eliminated or suppressed through the evolution of canonical Judaism and Christianity, although such elements survived through the mystical teaching of the Jewish Kabbalistic tradition (538 B.C. to A.D 70) and the Christian gnostic versions of creation and God (circa A.D. 200). According to Singer, the spiritual force for creativity described in the Kabbalistic literature is represented by a divine androgyny who embodies both the masculine and feminine qualities of the soul. As such, Singer contends that:

> The Kabbalah reformulates the entire Genesis story of Creation in terms of the *Sefiroth*, the ten mystical numbers or emanations of light that streamed forth from the original point of light . . . *Justice* and *Mercy*, in the sefirotha scheme, represent feminine and masculine elements, respectively, and so it is clear that without a harmonious balance between these two, the world could not have been created. (1972:161)

Similarly, Pagels maintains that the gnostic tradition in Christianity offers an important place to the feminine in early Christian teachings. The gnostic manuscripts, which are associated with a heretical tradition in Christianity, include a direct reference to God the mother and God the father, a masculine and feminine divinity that is closely related to the androgynous figure of the Kabbalah. In the gnostic teachings, the god figure is a dyad. Here the creative force is described as "a great power, the Mind of the Universe, which manages all things, and is a male . . . the other a great intelligence . . . is a female which produces all things" (Pagels, 1981:60). Other scriptures suggest that the Holy Spirit of the trinity is symbolic of the divine mother, the spirit who is "the mother of everything, for she existed before them all . . . " (Pagels, 1981:62).

One interpretation of both gnostic Christianity and Kabbalistic Judaism is that the theology of androgyny evolved out of the preexisting pagan goddess tradition and represents a desire to retain the feminine aspects of spirituality as patriarchal monotheism became more predominant. The evidence here is still somewhat speculative, yet it is possible to consider the development of spiritual consciousness as a transition from goddess worship and a feminine notion of creativity to god worship and a masculine definition of spiritual union, a perspective that is developed by Wilber in his discussion of the change from mother consciousness to father consciousness in the religious theology of the Western world. In Wilber's view, the advent of patriarchal religion contained elements of both evolutionary change as well as suppression of the feminine:

> Speaking in the most general terms, there is no question but that historically the major sphere of consciousness denied access to the feminine principle by the newly emergent patriarchy was that of socio-cultural communication; i.e. free mental exchange, free access to heaven, free ideation. The feminine principle was denied access to the newly emergent mind. (1981:232)

Evidence of a female-oriented spiritual consciousness is found in the analyses of ancient religious mythology (Ruether, 1977; 1985) and in the anthropological literature that focuses on the existence of goddess-worshipping societies which predate the advent of the Hebrew God in the Middle East (Berger, 1985; Gimbutas, 1980). Pamela Berger, for example, traces the evolution of the goddess from grain protectress to saint, concluding that:

> Since women, like the land, were seen as the primary source of life, most agriculturalists envisioned a female deity, an earth mother goddess, as the creative power behind all animal and plant fertility. . . .
> Different cultures had different appellations for this female personification and through this figure represented more than just the image of motherhood. . . . She was envisioned as having divine aspects and functions. As a multifaceted goddess she not only controlled the changing seasons but was sovereign over the underworld as well. It was, however, in the realm of birth, regeneration and plant fertility that her cult was mainly centered. (1985:5)

Similarly, Rosemary Radford Ruether (1977) has traced the development of the feminine in religious consciousness through the embodiment of Wisdom as female in the Old Testament and the evolution of Mariology in Christianity. More recently, she (1985) has undertaken a reevaluation of creation mythology from the Near East and Greek world. Beginning with a prebiblical time frame (4,000 B.C.), Ruether chronicles a process of increasing patriarchalization which is evident in the diminished role that the female assumes in creation mythology. Of this trend, she writes:

> In these accounts we can see a progressive trend toward the subordination and finally elimination of the female deities in cosmogenesis. The merging male creator God, who displaces the Goddess, comes to be seen as eternal, originating before cosmogenesis rather than being generated within it. The imagery of creation shifts from procreation to that of artisan tool making and verbal fiat. The world comes to be seen as something "created" outside the Creator from alien and different "stuff" rather than a procreative process by which gods are gestated within the body of the Primal Mother. (1985:38)

As these findings establish and substantiate the existence, importance, and suppression of goddess worship, it is not unreasonable to assume that spiritual consciousness within early human societies took the form of unification with the Mother, the feminine, or the Great Goddess as she was called. Thus, it is not unlikely that the symbiotic interpretation of religious experience was not at first genderless as Pollock maintains, nor only masculine as Freud suggests, but was initially female-oriented. As the role of creator shifted, however, from the mother to the father in religious thought, the object of unification in consciousness shifted from the feminine to the masculine. Thus, ultimate power, the realm of the divine and immortality, came to be associated with patriarchy. As such, the relationship between transcendence (spiritual fulfillment) and charisma is primarily understood and experienced in Western society as the union of the spiritual self with the masculine god figure, the disciple with the teacher. Further, as this is achieved within the context of small group commitment, the distinction between "heavenly" father and paternal parent becomes blurred.

The Charismatic Bond and the Quest for Paternalism

With the advent of monotheistic patriarchal religion, representations of God in the unconscious became associated with male-identified ego ideals who replace the archaic mother as the source of wholeness and fulfillment. The gender shift evident in such a process of transference reflects a pattern of male dominance in a culture where fathers are for the most part absent from the affective domains of familial bonding. As Nancy Chodorow points out in her analysis of "Family Structure and Feminine Personality" (1974), the division of labor by gender in industrialized societies results in family arrangements that allocate primary responsibility to women for child development and socialization. Because of limited male participation in child rearing, boys are deprived of a gender-identified role model with whom they can develop strong emotional ties, while girls are often sex-typed through limited interactions with the father in the family (Johnson, 1986). The effect of the patriarchal family structure, according to Chodorow, is that male children have difficulty developing a sense of self in the female world of childhood and thus form a masculine ego identity through denial and devaluation of the mother and that which is associated with the feminine in culture. The process of individuation for male children thus relies heavily on separation from the mother, a psychological rejection that is necessitated by the absence of the father in emotional development.

In applying Chodorow's theory to a wider cultural context, it can be argued that the effects of gender roles within the family have had far-reaching consequences which have influenced, among other social phenomena, the development of patriarchal religious traditions. As masculine ego development is dependent on separation from the first object of love, the mother, the historical rejection of maternal divinity may in part derive from this unconscious drive which is expressed through the desire of male culture to establish and maintain the paternal god as the ultimate source of creation. Accordingly, the predominance of patriarchal charismatic movements is one manifestation of the desire to retain a masculine definition of spiritual power through preserving a sphere of male control which is separate and distinct from the primacy of maternal dependence.

Further, the absence of the father figure in the patriarchal family also contributes to the need for religious movements that can provide a means through which the ideal father may be realized in the person of the charismatic leader who represents a transcendental father with the qualities of spirituality as well as familial paternalism. In effect, the relationship with the charismatic leader offers a father substitute (Downton, 1973) through which unconscious fulfillment can be achieved within the parameters of male bonding with a patriarchal god figure. The spiritual father offers the male devotee an affirmation of self and at the same time provides a role model on which to project the ego ideal. This view of male bonding and spirituality helps to explain the gender differences discussed earlier wherein male devotees were found to experience religious phenomena in far greater numbers than female devotees. In this regard, the significance of ego construction would appear to bear heavily on the process of merging with the charismatic leader. In traditional family arrangements, it is the women who are assumed to have weaker ego boundaries because of the primary relationship to the female caretaker who is undifferentiated for the female child. In this regard, Chodorow maintains:

> As long as women mother, we can expect that a girl's preoedipal period will be longer than that of a boy and that women more than men will be more open to and preoccupied with those very relational issues that go into mothering—feelings of primary identification, lack of separateness or differentiation, ego and ego boundary issues, and primary love not under the sway of the reality principle. (1979:110)

In the religious family, by comparison, it is men whose ego boundaries become blurred in the identification with the dominant paternal god figure. As the experience of conversion parallels primary socialization, it is now a male rather than female who is experienced as the creative progenitor and the primal affective relationship. As such, male devotees are more likely to merge completely, experiencing the mystical revelation of the undifferentiated self in connection to the all powerful spiritual father. Female devotees, on the other hand, have more difficulty projecting the ego ideal onto a masculine love object, as the nature of their relationship is not only defined by gender differences but by gender roles which are hierarchical.

In the fundamentalist groups such as charismatic Christian movements and Krishna Consciousness, women are isolated and segregated because of their association with flesh and sinfulness and therefore have greater obstacles to overcome in achieving spiritual union. Alternatively, in groups where sexuality is tied to spiritual development, such as the Tantric traditions described earlier, the women assume the role of consort, the vehicle through which the males achieve a state of spiritual power. Theoretically, the women might experience spiritual insight as well through sexual relations. However, this was generally not the case in the accounts of female devotees. For the most part, the women reported that rather than spiritually enlightened, they felt used and exploited by a system that linked sexual development to sexual service to the guru and his male followers.

This finding is particularly important in that existing research (Hood & Hall, 1980) on gender differences in mystical experience suggest that women tend to describe religious phenomena in erotic terminology which is receptive in nature. According to this view, the language of female mysticism expresses a sense of being entered by the object of spiritual unification. Thus the researchers conclude that in the realm of fantasy and the unconscious the experience of mystical revelation is eroticized by women. By contrast, the findings presented here indicate that when such unions are actualized through sexual relations with charismatic god figures, the erotic experience, while providing a sense of intimacy with the divine, is often carried out through a context of subordination characteristic of heterosexual norms in male-dominant culture. In analyzing the effects of eroticizing spirituality, it is therefore important to distinguish between submissive and nonsubmissive merging with God. For the female devotees, sexual unions with the leader and male disciples were experienced primarily as the former and were therefore bounded by the limits of a male spiritual hierarchy.

Further, the findings with respect to the frequency and type of male merging in charismatic movements challenges Hood and Hall's conclusions concerning greater female religious sensitivity. Their interpretive framework maintains that the erotic dimension of spirituality is more socially acceptable to women because of the predominance of the masculine god image, whereas the notion of spiritual union is problematic for men because of the homosexual overtones associated with a male god. For the men in this study, mystical revelation through merging with the charismatic leader was expressed primarily in filial terms that did not seem to engender homosexual conflicts or concerns. These findings therefore give support to the view that religious experience in patriarchal traditions is derived from identification of father with son, as the notion of the Trilogy implies, a social construction of spirituality that creates barriers rather than opportunities for female transcendence.

5.

Total Deconversion
The Rejection of the
Spiritual Father

The destruction of the idealized father image internalized by the devotee signifies a move toward total deconversion. In this study, 57 percent of the respondents separated from the leader after a period of ambivalence and indecision characterized by emotional upheaval, fear, and finally rejection of the leader and his world view. As the psychological bonding suggests, the act of separation is a difficult one, involving conflicting feelings that surround the need for autonomy and the simultaneous desire to remain merged with the spiritual parent. The tensions created during this stage of conscious choice and unconscious yearnings are manifested in a struggle of individuation through which the devotee restructures his or her ego boundaries. The ambivalence associated with this aspect of disengagement is illustrated in the following account, as a young male devotee agonizes over his decision to leave the guru:

> I had been in the movement four and a half years and I was trying to decide what to do. I was miserable and again I had found myself at a crossroads. I thought I had made my decision. I wasn't going back. But I still wasn't sure. Then I had this kind of vision. It was like daydreaming only very intense and I could have stopped it and brought myself to consciousness if I wanted but it would have been difficult. It was much more intense than a normal daydream but not so out of control as a dream. In it, the guru and all of his devotees were gathering around and they were all going to leave the world and go into heaven. And the guru had all his followers there and I asked if I could go and he told me, no, you can't because you have

placed yourself where I am no longer your guru, which is something he would say, a direct quote from his lectures.

He talked of people who leave and he said I have tried to bring them back but they reached a point where they had placed themselves where I am no longer their guru, their god. They are lost and they don't have me anymore and that's it. And he said all of this to me. And I asked him, I told him I would do anything he wanted if only he would take me back and I wanted to come with him and it was like the last chance so to speak. He said, yes, there is something you can do. You can acknowledge that I am the one true lord of the universe and all the other things, all the spiritual things, political stuff and school that I had been doing, none of that mattered. It was totally useless and I had to give it up.

And at that time there was a part of me that felt, yes, I would say anything and I sort of flashed back to when I first joined and the point of the whole thing was that you'd say anything. They say are you willing to give up your life for the lord? And you say, yes, and to a large extent I pledged myself to things I didn't absolutely believe at the time. But I did so for the promise of the cookies, the blissful experience. And there was part of me that would have done it again, said what he wanted even though I wasn't 100% sure. I wanted to be with him, to go to heaven, to experience his love. But another part of me said, no. In this vision, he said good-bye and they all floated off into heaven and I tried to follow them and I couldn't and I was left feeling very desolate and then I came back, so to speak, to normal consciousness and I was extremely depressed.

As this devotee retold his experience, he spoke of the cruelty of the vision and the cruelty of a god who would leave him behind, suffering in loneliness.

Because of the emotional nature of charismatic bonding, separation from the leader requires a change in consciousness on the part of the devotee which develops out of emerging doubts concerning the leader's godliness and unconditional love. For those followers who are in close proximity to the leader, the difficulty of maintaining the ideal is often greater as the more privileged disciples have the opportunity to witness the leader under stress or in moments of vulnerability. Here a devotee describes the contradictions as he perceived them:

The festivals sometimes made me sick. I think the other premies felt this way also. The Maharaj Ji, sitting in his picture frame on the window sill, the person in the picture frame can be anything you want him to be. Perfect, he is perfect. He is the lord, the guru. When you actually see him in person, he is not so perfect and it brings a lot of confusion. I used to do security at the Divine Light Mission and I was behind the scenes. And I would see him sometimes behind the scenes and it was very disturbing. I am not discounting that the guru was human but the actions I saw were not the actions of a Realized Being that he was supposed to be. Not one of the compassionate, loving fatherly figure.

At the festivals I would watch him sit in his chair, ready to receive the premies who would come to kiss his feet. He wasn't ready for the followers to kiss him. He was very nervous. He couldn't stop moving. He didn't recognize any of us. He didn't say hello or how are you. He was not very peaceful. He was very freaked out in a way. And he was yelling at the others, even shaking some of them. It was very weird you know. And then a few minutes later he was sitting up on the stage. I saw premies practicing the knowledge that he was teaching and they would say it was okay that he was so nervous. But I actually saw him being nervous and it is not what I think a godly figure would be in that situation.

But I don't want to discount that he might be someone who is in touch with a higher energy. That could be his personality, his make-up, the way he deals with his physical life. I'm not saying, well, see that, he is not divine. It just doesn't seem right to me to experience that.

The reaction of this devotee to the stress exhibited by the guru under pressure speaks to the continual conflict that converts experience in trying to discern what is true, what is real, and what are justifiable actions of the spiritual leader. As proof of divinity is often judged against the behavior of the spiritual teacher, the religious organization may seek to limit glimpses into the private moments of the leader's life that could lead to doubt about his godliness. This is a significant point in understanding the dynamic of charismatic bonding. While it is the personal environment of religious movements which allows for the development of strong affective bonds between the devotee and the leader, this familial closeness also provides an environment in which to observe and witness the behavior of the spiritual teacher and, as in the case of the Divine Light follower, to obtain a view of "God" which is both disappointing and disheartening.

In assessing the ways in which the leader assumes a more human character and a less godly demeanor in the minds of devotees, it is clear that there are specific issues, as in the process of social disaffection, around which disillusionment and doubt develop. Wright (1983:144) labels this aspect of disaffection as the conflict which emerges over "inconsistencies between the actions of the leaders and the ideals they symbolically represent." According to his findings on religious defection, this factor is the most important influence in determining separation from the group. The data reported here suggest that rejection of the leader can be linked to doubts which arise over questions of lifestyle, abuse, loss of love, and spiritual truth. These are categorized in Table 3 according to the percentage of devotees who expressed dissatisfaction in these areas. Yet unlike the separation from the social group, the break with the charismatic leader involves feelings of betrayal and the violation of trust as the object of love and devotion proves to be less than the ideal upon which the charismatic bond was established.

TABLE 3

Sources of Disaffection from the Charismatic Leader according to the Percentage of Devotees Expressing Disillusionment with His Actions

	Physical *Abuse*	*Psychological* *Abuse*	*Emotional* *Rejection*	*Spiritual* *Betrayal*
N = 40				
	31%	60%	45%	33%
	N = 12	N = 24	N = 18	N = 13

Abusive Practices

The relationship between abuse and love appears to be a pervasive characteristic of small-group commitment. In the charismatic Christian groups, physical abuse is often justified by a norm of discipline within the religious family that "requires" the spiritual father to punish and control his children in order to secure their relationship to God. According to a number of Christian followers, physical punishment was often used to save one's soul or to set an example for others who might stray. In one instance, a young male devotee was physically assaulted while living in a fundamentalist church in California. When he entered the movement, the leader offered him shelter in exchange for work and religious commitment:

> The pastor had a goal for changing Santa Monica, turning Santa Monica for Jesus. I thought that was very noble. He took me in and I stayed with them for at least two months. He was very strict. Of all the places I've gone, I considered that the best church. People listen to the leader because they believe from certain teachings in the Bible that the leader must be obeyed.
>
> In Santa Monica I was living in a dormitory in the basement of the church that had just been set up. You had to work and they paid you $75 a month. I was doing maintenance around the church grounds and I was attending church every night. But sometimes I would get homesick. And one day, on my day off, I was just lazing about. For some reason I was feeling really down and I had a couple of rock and roll tapes down in the dormitory. I came back to the room and I was feeling almost suicidal and I talked to a leader and I broke down and cried. And I told him I had a couple of rock and roll tapes in the dorm. He physically dragged me down into the dorm and he made me get them out and he started screaming at me about how evil they were and about bringing evil into the church and he threw them down and started stamping on them. And he ordered me to go and throw them out so I did and I was scared to death. I didn't want to go back inside because I thought he was going to beat me. But I threw them out and when I came back inside, it was like Dr. Jekyll and Mr. Hyde. He comes over to me and he is very big and he says stand up and I thought, this is it . . . and he hugs me. I couldn't believe it.
>
> I couldn't take a person like that. I felt loved by him because he was concerned about me. But the thing was he was concerned about his church. One of the powerful attractions is the idea of being loved.

In another charismatic group, a devotee who was very committed to the pastor began to question his holiness when the teacher insisted on maintaining total control over the lives of his followers:

> Pastor Jim was feared and revered. He was the leader of the thing. He was responsible for bringing them together. Pastor Jim's word was law. And if there was a question about how I raise my child, he was a strong disciplinarian. You can beat those kids till they are black and blue, that's all right. They are going to be the better for it. And people would do it because Pastor Jim said so. He was parental advisor and marriage counselor. And to

a great degree, he was responsible for who married whom. The women were submissive. They take the Bible view of it, plain and simple. And if the children said a naughty word or someone disobeyed, spank them or give them a bloody nose, that's all right. He was the man responsible for organizing it.

The people followed him completely, worshipped him. For eight years he ran the place totally. He made the decisions and when anyone challenged him, he would say that they were in with the devil, the cloak of evil had been pulled over their eyes.

It was hard for me to leave. I would go and talk with him and he would encourage me to stay on the farm. I had a lot of respect for him. The only thing that made me think twice or question his godliness was that he would never say that it was he who made this decision or that decision. When he would change his mind about something, he would say that the Holy Spirit had directed him to change. Maybe he should consider that it was his battle with right and wrong, good and evil. It is a problem when people are trying to do something spiritual and the human gets in the way.

Abusive practices within the Eastern-based groups generally took on a different meaning, as physical and psychological punishment were tied to the act of surrender and a test of commitment. In these circumstances, followers would be judged according to their willingness to endure pain and humiliation for the leader. Thus, Divine Light followers spoke of times when the guru would kick a groveling devotee or force liquids down a person's throat for the purpose of proving that he or she would do anything for the lord. In the following example of a small Buddhist community, a female devotee described her disillusionment with the guru as the result of a public incident that left her feeling confused and unsure of the kind of demands that complete surrender entailed.

This particular incident took place at a party that was given during seminary, a three-month retreat that is held annually. During the course of the evening, the guru noticed that two people were missing from the festivities. He ordered that they be brought by force from their rooms and publicly stripped. The teacher then paraded other naked devotees on his shoulders and became physically brutal with some of the participants. The respondent reported that some devotees, like herself, stayed on the sidelines and watched while the majority of followers were totally involved with the escalating intensity of the party activity. It was then that she experienced a turning point in her commitment to the teacher:

> The thing that I had most difficulty with was when I went to seminary, which is where the Tantric teachings are first taught. And they are incredible. I was pregnant at the time and for some reason, with the situation at seminary, I failed to grasp something there. And I see that as the very beginning of my slipping away. I can't put my finger on what happened exactly. But my failure to connect at that point was crucial.
>
> Tantra means you have to leave everything you've always believed in, every connection, everything you have ever held back and you must take a tremendous leap in possibilities. And I just wasn't ready to do that. I think a great many people make that leap. In this particular seminary because of an incident that happened at a party, there were a lot of people who sort of got mixed up and there was a moment's hesitation. Some of them worked it out and some of them didn't. I was one of the ones who didn't. What it amounted to was holding back. It was a situation where you had to leap ahead, have a great deal of faith in your teacher and what he was doing. People were able to do that. I was sort of able to do that mentally but not emotionally because I didn't want to get involved in what was going on. I can remember sitting in a chair very stiffly and watching the goings on and feeling like an outsider.

After seminary, this devotee continued to feel like an outsider, someone who could participate in the ritual but who no longer believed in the guru as she had before. Yet, despite the loss of trust in her spiritual teacher, this devotee felt that it was she who could not make the leap, surrender at a level where she too could strip naked and parade with the other followers who did not question the guru's authority, even in the face of violence and cruelty.

While physical abuse was experienced by 31 percent of the devotees in the study, representing a fairly even distribution among Christian and Eastern-based groups, psychological abuse was reported by 60 percent of the religious converts who described incidents involving verbal attacks that left the follower feeling inferior and with little self-esteem. As one devotee described the process, "it was an assault on our consciousness."

Members of a number of Eastern-based groups, including Divine Light Mission, Sikh, and Buddhist organizations, reported incidents in which they had been berated or had witnessed others who had been subject to strong criticism from the leader.

In discussing this aspect of disillusionment, devotees would often express a certain amount of anxiety, an uneasiness about sharing these innermost feelings of doubt and negativity concerning the spiritual teacher. In many cases, a visible increase in tension would become apparent during that part of the interview when a respondent discussed his or her feelings concerning the leader. Often there were long pauses between responses and a hesitancy to say what the devotee was thinking. In at least five interviews, the respondent only felt free to discuss the leader openly after the tape recorder had been turned off, as the following interchange illustrates:

> Interviewer: How did you feel about the teacher? Respondent: This is hard to answer. The negative aspect of my membership in the group was the male leadership. This is very difficult for me to talk about because I feel I am talking about someone who is seen to have a very high spiritual being and to sit here and tell you what I feel about something within him is very difficult because I have this other side of me that runs the tape, the other trip, the spiritual path. I feel almost sacrilegious . . . Maybe if you could turn off the tape recorder . . . [tape recorder is turned off]. Now I feel a lot better about talking about it . . . [a long pause]. Well, the teacher treated people very badly. I just couldn't take it. I know it is part of the act of losing the ego, an important process but he would be so abusive, telling us we had no value that we were unworthy and pitiful. He only contributed to a low self esteem and I could not accept this man of God, even with his spirituality. The pattern of abuse was just too much for me.

Throughout the interview process, it became apparent that negative thoughts about the leader induced feelings of anxiety, fear, and concern for speaking aloud what had been private doubts and secret suspicions. By participating in the study, the respondents chose to reveal themselves and yet for 80 percent of the followers, it was the first time that they had told someone else that they had questioned "God." In some ways the interview itself seemed almost like a confession, a public admission that they had been involved in a religious movement, that they had accepted God, and now they were rejecting Him, openly and publicly to a researcher. For many, this process seemed to be another step in disaffection, in separating completely from the former religious tie.

In terms of the actual incidents of psychological abuse, both men and women reported feelings of low self-esteem, particularly as the leader reminded them of how far they were from attaining the ego ideal. In this aspect of commitment as in most others, sex differences were evident in the types of violations committed by the devotees. Men might show a lack of self-discipline and religious devotion, whereas women were subject to verbal attacks on their purity, morality, and sinfulness. Among the female devotees, 68 percent reported these abusive practices by the leadership. In one Christian group, for example, a female devotee was told that she needed to be delivered from her sins. Following this declaration, she was chastised publicly for having "the spirit of homosexuality" because of her close relations with other female members. A few weeks later, she was again called before the group and this time she was delivered from the "spirit of lust" because she had been seen talking to too many male devotees. When this young woman sought to leave the group, she was told that Satan would do terrible things to her family and when she finally made the break, she described herself as suicidal, confused, humiliated, and depressed.

Another charismatic Christian follower reported similar feelings of depression, confusion, and suicide. Throughout her six-year association with the church, she had been told repeatedly by the pastor that she concentrated too much on the flesh and not enough on the spirit. She was accused of lustful behavior and criticized for being an improper wife and mother. In this case, the church had forbidden the devotee to work, although she maintained that her husband was not providing well enough for the family. The church did not approve of wives who worked outside the home and the pastor told this woman that her desire to find a job was a reflection of her worldly and material greed rather than of real family need. Other more godly female members were held up as the ideal to which she should aspire. Ultimately, the conflict was too great for her. She described her leaving in this way:

> It was an accumulation of I can't live like this any more. I can't live and
> pretend I am a godly woman, righteous and as pure as snow. It was like I
> was in a glass closet and the walls were getting smaller. I couldn't breathe.

Finally, one clear example of the type of denigration to which many
of the women were subjected took place within a small Bahai sect that
was led by one man who interpreted the scriptures for a small group of
followers. In this situation, a young university student reported the following incident which led to her leaving the movement.

> In the Bahai faith there is a council which is there to help you if you cannot
> keep the laws of the faith. One law is that of chastity. I went to the council
> with my problem. I wanted to live with a male friend of mine. A few weeks
> before, another member, a man, had gone before the council with the same
> situation. He wanted to live with a woman even though they weren't mar-
> ried. This man said he could not keep the chastity laws. Greg, the leader of
> the group, told this man that the decision was between himself and God.
> Sex was, after all, a natural male desire and it was understandable that he
> would want this relationship.
>   A few weeks later, I went before the council fully expecting the same
> consideration. But this time Greg yelled at me and screamed at me. He told
> me I was immoral and sinful, that women must be obedient and adhere
> strictly to the laws of God. I was told I would be ostracized and ridiculed. It
> was then I made the decision to leave. But still Greg threatened me with
> expulsion. He said he would write to the central Bahai organization and
> ask that I be expelled on moral grounds. Then he put a notice in the na-
> tional newsletter condemning my behavior.

The abusive practices of the leader result in the painful recognition that in
His wisdom and holiness, God the Father could also be a cruel and vindic-
tive person. For many devotees, this disenchantment was expressed not
only as betrayal but as rejection and disappointment; a feeling that because they had been hurt and bruised by the leader, they were not loved as
they should have been.

Rejection and Loss of Love

In the study as a whole, 45 percent of the devotees expressed explicit
disappointment with the emotional dimension of the leader-follower re-

His name has remained a mantra of my heart. A long time has passed and he has never acknowledged me. He will not love me. He will never love me.

That final acknowledgment, that the devotees will never be loved by the teacher, is perhaps the most hurtful realization of all, the turning point from hopefulness to disillusionment. In the case above, rape and degradation were perceived as a test of love and devotion, an ultimate act of faith that alienated this young woman even further from her teacher and left no doubt that he had, after all, rejected her for her weakness. For other converts, the betrayals were perhaps less harsh, repeated violations of faith by the leader who ignored his disciples, who abused them, and left them wanting more than he could possibly give to all those who sought his affection, protection, and knowledge.

In one final example of rejection and loss, a Hare Krishna devotee describes her love for her teacher and the loss she experienced when she discovered his relationship with other female devotees:

I really loved him. It was a heartfelt thing. I never had any sexual relationships before that. I never had any boyfriends like in high school. All of my friends were the kind of friends you could relate heart to heart with. So I had no sexual relationship with my teacher. I guess I was kind of afraid of it. I didn't want to deal with the consequences of it. He never really noticed me. He kept me happy. I was so tight with this guy. He really loved me. One time he said I was more like a wife to him than his real wife. He would talk to me and tell me his problems. He liked the women and he liked taking care of them but he said it was hard.

It turned out later that he was having sex with many of the women in the party. But I didn't know it. Because I wasn't into that. For me it was a much more pure thing and I didn't know he was having sex with them and everything. When they found out he was sleeping with all the other women, the party broke up and I was heartbroken.

But when the party broke up and all this came out about how he was sleeping with all the other women, I was so depressed I walked around dazed. I couldn't see straight. I couldn't chant my rounds. They started a new women's party with a woman in charge and I told her I was in love with the leader and that I didn't think I could love anyone anymore. I was holding all of it in and hadn't really grieved yet. I didn't know who I was anymore.

lationship. These religious converts often spoke in terms of the pain of
unrealized love or the rejection they experienced at the hands of an insen-
sitive god. After four years of intermittent abuse within the religious
movement, one devotee said, "I feel an emptiness inside me sometimes
for somebody to love me. But I don't think I ever felt that God really
loved me like He was supposed to."

The story of Sheila, a devotee quoted in a previous chapter, is among
the most painful of all the accounts told by respondents. While she was a
member of an Eastern-based group, she was raped by three strangers, an
incident for which Sheila was later blamed by her spiritual teacher. Eventually she left the group dispirited and confused. During the interview she
spoke of the Yogi who still invaded her consciousness and who remained
in her thoughts, dominating her emotions. Still troubled by her seven-
year commitment to the movement, she retold her experience in a stream-
of-consciousness fashion, repeating over and over again how deeply she
had loved the guru but how she could no longer sustain a relationship to a
god who clearly did not want her:

> I was raped by three men and I endured it, believing that this was in
> some way a test planned by my spiritual teacher. They were strangers in a
> city where I had gone; I had been sent away from the ashram. I had been
> walking and I was very tired. A man offered me a ride and I accepted. At
> first I gave myself in gratitude to this man but then the others came and I
> was forced. I was handed down like a thing. I was not someone who was
> giving, I was a thing being used with no identity or feeling. There was
> nowhere to go. I didn't know how to get out of the road. I talked to God
> and I chanted the whole time it happened.
>
> After the rape I became a nonperson. I was made to feel low and
> unworthy, like an untouchable, disgusting. It hurt so much. The vanity of a
> man who can't accept one flaw in a woman. The vanity of a man who
> exploits women, the vanity of a man who dwells on the one thing that is not
> perfect in the woman and uses her as a doormat, that vanity is called spiri-
> tual teacher.
>
> If I could stop remembering what happened, stop remembering the
> mental presence, my suffering would be over. But there was an Indian Sikh,
> my spiritual teacher, who really spoke to my soul. His name became the
> mantra of my heart. I thought he would free me but he steals in the face of
> love. We are taught, cater to his ego, cater to his ego, cater to his ego . . .

For this devotee in particular, her relationship to the guru was couched in the imagery of pure, chaste, and unconditional love. Thus romantic notions of honor, protection, and care sometimes infuse the spiritual bond. Within this added source of idealization, the effect of the leader's betrayal can be devastating as his actions violate the sanctity of the special relationship between the convert and her spiritual mentor.

Spiritual Betrayal

For a third of the respondents, disappointment with the charismatic leader focused on spiritual disillusionment and the contrast between the ideal of godliness and the reality of the guru's actions and lifestyle. In this regard, doubts would arise over the leader's ability to provide a spiritual environment as questions developed about men of God who have sexual relations with their devotees, who live in mansions and drive Rolls Royces, and who can spare little time for the spiritual connection for which devotion has been given. A good case in point is the experience of Seth, a Buddhist convert who joined the movement when it was first established as a small community in New England. Here he traces his conversion and the changes that took place over time which led to his leaving and separation from the spiritual teacher:

I discovered this group myself. I had done some readings of Tibetan Buddhism. When I joined I went up to the [farm]. What attracted me most was the mystical aspect. It was steeped in mysticism and reincarnation. I liked the guru's teachings but I was always embarrassed in his presence. I was never at ease. They said he could see through you and all that and with me there was a lot to see through. I stayed at the [farm] for four years and I was married there. Also it was there that the teacher made me a Buddhist in a ceremony that was just me.

But then we moved from the [farm] out West. The whole thing became less freaky and open and more formal and constricted. There were bowings and blessings and for years I resisted any sort of administration. I never had a meditation instructor, although I was one. I was never monitored and few people wanted to be my students. I started going to the university. I got a degree in philosophy and I began to see what was wrong with Buddhism, with [the guru] in particular. I had a long time to think it over and I did not formally separate until three or four years after I had begun to have my doubts.

When I started getting into rational thinking, I started thinking what is most vulnerable in Buddhism and I started thinking about the doctrine of reincarnation. Now specifically what I think is that he must be a liar since he said he is reincarnated, which is a very serious fault in my eyes and therefore he is a liar and putting people on.

He makes claims that could not possibly be true. And I believe that his lies are catching up with him, that his ability to live is degenerating. I personally feel his vision is not holding together as an Oriental psychologist who came to a group of pink delicate Westerners. He was great for four or five years, teaching as much as he could. But now I believe he is deceiving people—taking away their ability to live as human beings and believe you are going to be reincarnated.

A basic premise of Buddhism is that control is knowledge. If you can control yourself that's wisdom. There is a definite desire on the part of [the guru] to keep Buddhism going through the control over his disciples. It is a cult you know. They turned Buddhism into a cult. Everybody gets fat when [the guru] gets fat. Everyone drinks when [the guru] drinks. I go into a thousand dining rooms and they all have carpets that are just alike and they imitate him without thinking. And I don't believe he even practices Buddhism anymore. I don't think he really meditates. I think that some of the original things are just not there any more.

For this devotee, separation from the guru resulted from a spiritual reappraisal of his godliness that accompanied a breakdown in the personal dynamic between disciple and teacher. In becoming aware of the behavior of other converts, Seth recognized aspects of idolatry that he found both false and objectionable. More specifically, Seth saw the futility of sacrificing one's self so completely to another who may only be deceiving his followers. In effect, as the sense of deception deepens, the disaffected devotees see themselves as reflection of those who are still committed and in these mirror images they see the contradictions that a continued belief in the leader cannot dispel.

Among the more obvious contradictions are the lifestyles to which the leaders become accustomed as their power and influence grow. Especially in the Eastern-based groups, the guru represents a person who has transcended the profane and mundane aspects of life and yet once in the United States, the connection to materialism seems to transform what had been a more pure and spiritual movement in the East. Here this change is discussed by a Divine Light devotee who left the group after a twelve-year commitment:

> They told us that Maharaj Ji was bringing peace to this planet, but living in this age required airplanes and luxury hotels, the finest food in the world for the Lord, the finest clothing and everything which developed into thousands and thousands of people who were working their butts off, seven days a week. I sometimes feel in the beginning he was really sincere. When I first saw him he was really sincere. But I think a lot of it just came from being corrupted by the lifestyle. Even his personality decayed.

The luxury and indulgence that often characterizes the life of the religious leader is rarely enough in itself to create a crisis in faith. This reality, like the reality of abuse, contributes to a growing sense of disillusionment which is continually challenged by the desire to deny wrongdoing or culpability on the part of the charismatic leader. As one devotee explained, "Even after I knew, I just couldn't accept it all. I wanted to believe there was a reason he was doing what he was doing, that it was part of God's plan. But deep down inside I had to question what was going on and I had to face that maybe he was not god, maybe I was alone."

The fear of being alone, of losing what is potentially the most gratifying relationship of all, is a cause of continued dependence on the charismatic relationship. Even as the attributes of idealism and godliness are stripped away, the desire for continued connection and identification is not forsaken in a strong and passionate bid for autonomy. Rather, as the cases indicate, the process of severing the emotional bond is met with a psychological resistance to separation and rarely is total deconversion achieved without external reinforcement, either from loved ones, other former devotees, or new religious teachers to whom identification can be transferred.

External Reinforcement and Patterns of Reconversion

The breaking down of the idealized god image in the unconscious is facilitated by alternative sources of object love. The need for a "replacement object" can be understood in terms of Emerson's view (1962; 1969) of the nature of power in dependent relationships. According to the principles of social exchange elaborated by Emerson, the dependency of the devotee on the leader is inversely proportional to the availability of needs fulfillment through other means of affiliation and affective enclosure. Where such alternatives are not established, the likelihood of continued emotional dependency on the leader will be greater. As in the authority structures described by Goffman (1961), social control in the religious movements is therefore dependent on the psychological control associated with the leader's role as the exclusive object of primary love. Only as alternative associations become available to devotees, offering other means for emotional and spiritual fulfillment, is separation from the charismatic leader likely to occur.

The psychological nature of power-dependent relationships helps to explain the trend toward reconversion evident in the studies of religious movements. Consistent with the findings of other researchers in the field, 50 percent of the respondents interviewed here had become members of a new religious group after their disaffection or were in the process of changing their commitment at the time of the study. (This figure is quite a bit lower than the 78 percent reconversion figure reported by Wright in his study of religious defection.) In noting the pattern of reconversion, Richardson (1978) suggests that ours is an "age of conversion careers," drawing an analogy between the sequence of conversion experiences and serial monogamy in marriage. What should be emphasized, however, in the leader-follower dynamic is the importance of the spiritual connection. While other secular relationships, such as marriage and family, can offer social and emotional rewards, it is only the religious leader who can fulfill the desire to know and attain God, a desire that is not diminished by the failure of the conversion experience. Even among the most emotionally distraught respondents, there was no one who said, "there is no God, I just can't believe any more." Rather, the disillusionment was reflected specifically in their disappointment with the leader, feelings such as, "Is this what God is like? Is this a man of God?" The desire to continue the search and seek out a new religious perspective indicated time and again that the quest for love and understanding remains a fundamental part of the individual's life, not easily relinquished even in the face of great disappointment.

Perhaps of most interest here are the kinds of movements that replace the previous affective and spiritual ties. Contrary to the findings of Wright (1983) whose data suggest that the majority of former devotees reconvert to conservative fundamentalist groups, the results reported here indicate that the new affiliations selected by former devotees tend to be characterized by loosely structured organizations, with few hierarchical arrangements and a style of leadership that is less authoritarian in character. In four cases, the leader of the new movement was a woman, an interesting finding in view of the previous discussion on the significance of gender in religious experience. The respondents, two of whom were women and two of whom were men, spoke specifically of the gentleness and nurturing that the new group and the change to a female leader offered. Here a male devotee speaks of his new affiliation:

> I have become very suspicious of all dogmatic religions. I don't like dogmas, cults. I see what it leads to. The church I go to now is Hannah K. We go to her church every once in a while. She runs her own chapel of miracles. She is a psychic, a Christian psychic. Right now I feel there is a psychic realm. I have had a few psychic experiences. I haven't experienced it completely. I don't believe in it totally. I don't believe everything Hannah says *per se*, but it is a little more profound than mainstream religion.
> Her theological outlook is more holistic. It includes Christianity, Hinduism, and so on. Hannah treated my brother for terminal cancer and he survived a year more than the doctors said he would. My parents have seen her and they think she is terrific too. I started thinking about positive thinking and she has helped me to sort things out from my past.

In the following excerpt, a female devotee describes her bonding to a new guru, a man but a different kind of spiritual teacher who represents a less authoritarian religious path:

> I am now involved with Ram Dass. It is totally different now. Ram Dass has often said in public that he has no use for teachers in terms of subordination. Surrender on a spiritual level, perhaps, if it happens, but not on a material level. A teacher for him is another tool. I think that is the

correct understanding. I think there are a lot of reasons for my relationship with Ram Dass. I know he will never allow me to have an expectation that he will not fulfill. He will work with me through it.

I have never quit practicing, quit developing the spiritual side. I'm just one of those beings who will keep doing it. With Ram Dass it will be different. I had a vision that he would be my teacher. I am glad that Ram Dass loves me, real glad.

In one final example of a reconversion experience, a devotee talks about a movement with which he became involved after a three-year commitment to Divine Light Mission. By comparison, the new religious orientation has almost no structure and few demands:

After I left Maharaj Ji, I met some people who were doing things that attracted me. This group was following the teachings of Arvi Coshi, a man who brought some teachings back from India. He died last summer and there are some people doing his work, trying to apply what he talked about in his life. Basically, a Krishnamurti approach in a very intense and passionate way. We practice meditation and we have this guru who tells us that our mind is bad and we look and our mind is still there. What's going on? Can there be some clarity and sanity in this life? If some kind of clarity can develop then the mind can understand and once it is understood, it can be quiet and we experience something in that quietness. Basically that is what it is. There are no meetings. There is no organization. There is just these people who are doing work. They feel it is intense and important.

In the experiences of reconversion, the rejection of the religious community and the charismatic leader suggests a desire for a more maternal ideal of spirituality, one that embraces unconditional love, warmth, and compassion as opposed to the aggressive qualities of the masculine god/father. A follower of a charismatic Christian group discussed this aspect of his disillusionment:

I was very disappointed in the charismatic movement. I left in a total state of confusion and it has left a certain amount of scars so to speak. I was very angry with the pastor for his hold on the people at the church. He had absolute authority over every member and he was supposed to be the Word of God, a god that I just couldn't accept. He spoke of the prophecies and the world ending with war and pestilence; and the god of the Jews who massacred women and children in the Book of Joshua. That kind of god does not make sense to me. I am looking for a god of love.

Two other disciples, both men, spoke about their spirituality in terms of female relationality, the physical and emotional warmth they experienced through intimacy with the women in the movements which was absent from their relationship to the charismatic leader. Perhaps, then, in rejecting the authoritarian charisma of god the father, the disaffected devotees begin the search anew for a more feminine godliness. If so, the reconversion phenomena may represent a turning away from the primal father in the quest for the original object of love, the primal mother. In one sense then the continual search for the true religious path may be understood as the desire to rediscover that aspect of the feminine which has been lost through the development of spirituality under patriarchy.

This search for the feminine has been expressed in the growth of feminist alternatives to patriarchal religion. These spiritual alternatives, like the charismatic communities, emerged out of the upheaval of the 1960s, offering a variety of choices for those disillusioned with the traditional mainstream denominations and with what Emily Culpepper (1978) has termed the "pseudo newness" of the charismatic movements. Among the feminist alternatives to male-dominated religion there developed both a reformist approach as well as more revolutionary choices. The reformist tradition, characterized by the work of Ruether (1972) and Ellen Umansky (1985) seeks to reform the Judeo-Christian faiths to include equal participation of women and the acknowledgment of a feminine spirit. It is not, however, to the reformist tradition that defectors from charismatic groups have often turned. Rather, follow-up research (Jacobs, 1989) to this study suggests that women, disillusioned by their experiences with the new religious groups, frequently seek out the more radical feminist approaches found in the women's spirituality movement.

The women's spirituality movement is identified by the development of female-centered groups that are generally nonhierarchical in organization and legitimate the feminine principle in the concept of the divine. Often these groups are associated with contemporary forms of goddess worship such as those found in the practices of Wicce and the

Craft and with the work of revolutionary theologians such as Starhawk (1979; 1982) and Z. Budapest (1986). Their work focuses on the development of witchcraft as a contemporary religion through which women can identify with the goddess symbol and participate in life-affirming rituals that validate notions of female strength and creativity. Through field research in Colorado, it became apparent that women who participate in the female-centered spiritual communities are seeking nonpatriarchal and nonauthoritarian religious structures that offer a source of female bonding and spiritual visions of female strength. Many of these women reported that prior to their interest in women's spirituality, they had joined one of the new religious movements, most frequently a community that had an Eastern orientation which stressed individual growth and spiritual development. In rejecting these alternatives, the women spoke of the need for redefining their spiritual consciousness through a religious path that was female identified.

These devotees joined loosely organized women's groups whose communal orientation was structured primarily around female-centered rituals that form the basis for spiritual and social relations within the movement. What is of particular interest in these ritualistic practices is the significance of maternal imagery. In the rituals observed by this researcher, group members were led through guided meditations in which they were asked to envision themselves in some form of goddess imagery. In many of these visions a maternal theme was obviously present, as the following account suggests:

> The image that came to mind during the meditation was one of my own mother, someone very strong, wise, and nurturing. The goddess I experienced had a human form with human expressions—anger, warmth, nurturance, forgiveness. All these kinds of things I associate with women.

The visualization of the maternal imagery as described here contrasts with the internalization of the paternal god figure by charismatic devotees. The effect of this gender difference in the representation of the divine is to offer women that which is accessible to men in the charismatic communities, an ego ideal on which to project positive images of the self and the gender affirmation of the symbolic parent-child relationship. As a result, women in these groups reported that in comparison with their experience in patriarchal movements, they developed a growing sense of empowerment and an improved self-concept because of their participation in the women's spiritual communities. Thus, for some female devotees involvement in the charismatic group led to the rejection of male authority and the acceptance and legitimization of female definitions of power.

6.

Separation and the Redefinition of Social Reality

In the third and final stage of disengagement from the religious movement, the devotee begins to redefine his or her self-concept apart from the social community provided by the group and apart from the spiritual identification provided by the charismatic leader. Within the context of changing commitment, this process involves the rejection of a religious theology (intellectual disaffection), ethical structure, and deity concept that often leaves the converts feeling isolated, lonely, and unsure about the fundamental life questions for which they had sought answers through conversion. In effect, the world of total meaning which had been so carefully and completely constructed for the devotees proves to be a false and perhaps unworthy world view on which to base their lives and faith.

Having lost the security of social affiliation and faced with both the promise of personal autonomy and fear of it, the disaffected converts enter a period of transition immediately following their separation in which they reformulate their sense of self apart from their former religious commitment and personal identification with the charismatic leader. This process of disengagement is made especially difficult by the effects of merging on the individual. Here a female devotee describes her struggle to differentiate:

110

> I wanted to leave but I couldn't find an apartment on my own. That was part of my symbiotic enclosure. I could not emotionally separate. . . . I could not leave. Psychologically I was not only traumatized but I was experiencing some sort of symbiotic enclosure. I don't know if it was psychological or spiritual. I was not able to construct my own existence.

The trauma of separation among religious devotees has been compared to the sense of dislocation experienced by individuals undergoing divorce (Skonovd, 1981; Wright, 1983). The parallel between divorce and disaffection is not surprising in light of the intense affective bonding that characterizes both the commitment of religious affiliation and the commitment of marital relationships. In both circumstances, the severing of bonds leads to a reassessment of one's personal identity outside the context of an emotional relationship which had previously provided a source of ego identification for the individual. In marriage it is the spouse to whom a part of the self has been sacrificed in love; in conversion it is the charismatic leader to whom surrender has been given. Thus, throughout the period of separation, the conflict and challenge of self-definition is common to both experiences.

While marital separation offers one means to understand the emotional upheaval characteristic of deconversion, perhaps a more informative analogy is offered by Levine (1984) who suggests that leaving religious movements is reminiscent of growing up and separating from one's parents. Disengaging from the leader involves rejecting the idealized parent as the devotee suffers both the death of an ideal and the loss of a source of intense love and devotion. The initial phase of leaving is thus characterized by feelings of isolation and loneliness which are intensified by a period of grief and self-blame.

Isolation and Loneliness

In establishing life outside the movement, converts experience loneliness and isolation; their inner psychic life is no longer defined by the spiritual consciousness of the religious theology and the shared world view of other group members. This sense of isolation is often exacerbated by the social adjustment a devotee must make as he or she reenters the less rigid and unstructured world outside the movement. This period of adjustment is especially difficult for those devotees who have lived in the religious community, whether in ashrams or church facilities. These devotees in particular (73% of the sample) often feel adrift, unsure of what they believe in, and uncomfortable with the outside world after leaving the cloistered environment of the religious group. Here one devotee describes this sense of isolation as he made the transition from a Christian religious community to a university setting:

> When I first came back, part of me still very much wanted to be at the farm. I was different. I had trouble with dorm life, the free sexuality of the women. I still felt like a missionary. I never cursed, never had a harsh word. I had been in a sterile environment for four months. I just didn't fit in with the college life of the dorms. I had a different perspective.

In this case the social aspects of reintegration involved reentry from the sheltered social system of the communal farm into the outer world, a transition that might be compared to the problems confronting the reintegration of war veterans, Peace Corps volunteers, and prison inmates into mainstream society. These special populations, like religious converts, experience the effects of resocialization as they first adapt to cultural norms within the group and then to the cultural norms outside the group once membership in the special population has been terminated. In categorizing the problems of transition common among inmates who are released from prison, Irwin (1970) describes an adjustment period not unlike that experienced by those who have been in religious movements, particularly devotees who have spent long periods of time in the communal setting of ashram life. According to Irwin,

> The first systematic attention to the special problems incurred by a population returning to its former social setting was directed toward English veterans of World War II who were being repatriated from war prisons or being discharged from overseas duty. Some attention was paid to the similar situation in America. Recently, the reentry problems of the Peace Corps returnees have been causing considerable concern.
> In all these instances the adjustment problems are seen to be complex,

involving extreme personal stress, psychological "symptoms," and problems of "resocialization," as well as the more obvious problems, such as locating employment. (1970:108)

For the religious convert, the psychological and social manifestations of isolation are often intensified by actual experiences of rejection that former devotees undergo as they separate from the movement. In 40 percent of the cases, respondents indicated that they felt ostracized by group members who had formerly been friends and confidants. Devotees would often report that as soon as they no longer attended church or lived within the ashram, they were rejected by those who remained committed. In some instances, for example, those who were involved in charismatic Christian groups, the ostracism was formalized as part of a religious mandate to shun sinners who had given up the true path. In the dormitories at the university, members of the Church of Christ would carry out this formal act of shunning by refusing to speak to disaffected devotees, to sit with them in public areas, or to acknowledge them in any way. One devotee reported that after he left the church, he was at first coerced by the others to come back and pray with them. When he refused, they said they would pray for his soul. But a week later these same concerned devotees avoided him completely:

> When I left I would talk to them and they would ignore me. I was not the one shunning them, they were shunning me. Whenever they see you, it's like, wow, look at the corpse that just crawled out of the grave. They don't say they are going to shun you but they do. You know these guys are supposed to be your best friends within the church so if you've made the mistake of dropping all your old friends like they tell you to, then you have no support to come back to after you leave.

In other cases, former devotees said that once their departure from the group became known among other members, they never heard from these people again. As one devotee describes this immediate isolation: "With them it was just a matter of one day I wasn't there any more. Nobody called and said, Can I help? What's going on? There was nothing of that sort."

For those followers who had been living in a communal or ashram-type setting, the sense of ostracism and loneliness was felt as soon as they moved out of the communal living situation. Among those who stayed in the environs where the group resided, the difficulty of transition was intensified by seeing other community members on the streets and in stores, receiving only slight recognition or acknowledgment that they had once been part of the same movement and had shared the same world view. For these disaffected devotees, one of the most difficult aspects of separation involved confronting those who remained within the group and whose love and care had been contingent upon group membership and a shared identity. "I would see the other followers on the street," a devotee said. "They would look away or avoid my eyes. They never asked why I left. They did not want to know." In the more extreme cases, this avoidance would also involve condemnation either as a lost soul or as a person who has lost his or her sanity. A year after she left, a former Buddhist still felt the pain of such labeling: "I'm still seen as someone in the community who went through a crazy experience. I still don't know how to make those people believe and understand what happened to me."

In about 25 percent of the cases, the ostracism felt by the former devotees was self-imposed. In these situations, the dynamic of rejection seemed to be initiated by the devotee rather than by his or her former group associates. As a necessary act of separation, these respondents spoke of an isolation they had chosen for themselves in order to break from the movement and from the ties that had kept them bonded to the group. Here a member of an Eastern-based group reflects on his negative feelings toward those who are still affiliated:

> The majority of my friends are still in the community. Just about everybody I see is a Buddhist or everyone I know. Mostly I sort of view them as jerks. It is really my problem not their problem. They would be just as friendly to me whether I was Buddhist or not. It really is my embarrassment. They don't feel one way or the other toward me.

A number of other devotees expressed a similar need to discredit and reject their former friends, a rejection that seemed to facilitate the rejection of that part of themselves that was still in any way identified with the leader. And yet, whether such ostracism was self-imposed or initiated by the group, the overwhelming feeling of the disaffected devotees was that of loss and sadness, a deep emotional response which in many ways is comparable to the adjustment that a battered child must make in his or her restructuring of the world outside the abusive family.

The Battered Disciple

Studies of psychologically and physically battered children (Barbino, Guttmen, & Seeley, 1986; Lowenstein, 1985) indicate that the manifestations of abuse are varied and include a range of psychological affects. Children in dysfunctional families suffer from low self-esteem, a negative view of the world, depression, and anger. They experience guilt for the failure of the parent relationship and a continuing sense of fear of punishment and rejection. Many of these same symptoms are present in the disaffected devotees. Immediately following departure from the movements, depression and guilt were among the most common feelings expressed over loss of the spiritual father and the security of his religious community. In two cases the devotees underwent hospitalization for the depression that had come to characterize their life outside the movement.

One woman reported: "For a period of time after I came out, I just quit feeling anything about God. I just wouldn't acknowledge that part of me and I went into the pits. I just went into the pits and I didn't function at all." Nine other respondents reported that they spent a period of time in which they felt detached from everything, dispirited, and unable to carry on with the day-to-day aspects of daily life.

Besides depression, feelings of guilt develop around leaving the charismatic leader, and the perceived failure to be a "perfect" and disciplined devotee. For some respondents the sense of guilt over separation was expressed as betrayal in leaving the leader, forsaking the father in a time of crisis. For other followers guilt was associated with making the transition to a secular life, as the authority and weight of God's laws hovered over their daily activities outside the movement. In one case, a Christian follower spoke of the guilt she felt right after she had left the small charismatic church. "I was afraid to dance, to take a couple of drinks, or even go to a movie. These were all activities that had been forbidden."

During such moments of doubt about separation, effects of the internalized god/father are manifested in fear of retribution. Even those devotees who were convinced that the leader was not directly connected to God often referred to the possibility that they might be wrong and if so, that they were doomed:

> It is possible that there is a Jehovah and that there is a hell and if the pastor is right then I don't have a chance in the world. I try not to think about that too much.

For many of the followers, the sense of dread that surrounds the leaving process is perceived in real rather than abstract terms as the disillusioned convert awaits a sign from God that he or she is now damned and lost forever. "I waited for my marriage to break apart," one devotee reported, while others spoke of expecting sickness or death for themselves or their loved ones:

> It was funny. I had all these taboos. Even as married couples you are not supposed to have sex except for procreation and then it was only once a month. We were living by that standard and it was like fire and brimstone if you break this taboo, the wrath of God will come down on you.

As internalized fear sustains the bond to the leader, devotees engage in risk-taking behaviors which challenge the omnipotent power of his authority. One male respondent began by violating a simple food taboo. When there was no apparent retribution, he risked another violation of the religious law and still nothing happened that he could attribute to God's wrath. Slowly, over time, he resumed a life that was not controlled by fear of sin and God, and thus he could entertain a freedom of choice that had not been possible while in the movement nor in the months immediately following his departure.

The actions and experiences of other disaffected devotees seem to play an equally important role in reconstructing a social reality that is not based on fear and dependence on the charismatic leader. One young woman described the reinforcement she found in witnessing the "fate" of others who had dared to leave:

> It's like when these people had left, I was just sort of waiting for when their doom would come. And it didn't come. Years later they still weren't doomed. And I went and talked to this one man. He was really nice and he told me that he thought the church was a cult. He said they don't accept you for what you are, you have to conform to their image and if you don't fit in, you have to make yourself fit in. And this man said he never felt better since he left and he was considered one of the worst sinners in the church. And God hadn't struck him down. As a matter of fact he was doing pretty well. He hadn't been hit by lightning and his kids weren't dead or anything. So I figured it was all right for me too.

As this account suggests, validation and encouragement from former devotees offers an important source of support in the transition phase of disaffection. This support is especially effective in validating feelings of doubt about the spiritual leader and in confirming perceptions of reality which question his claim to godliness. Deprogrammers are well aware of the effect that such reinforcement has on devotees who are wavering over their commitment. It is, in fact, common practice to employ former converts as deprogramming agents. Two persons who participated in this study were deprogrammed by an organized anti-cult network, although they returned to the movements afterward. In both cases, the converts described their deprogrammers as former devotees who had since "seen the light"; and it was their testimony that was most convincing:

> There was one thing that really struck me at the time of the deprogramming. The one deprogrammer from the Divine Light Mission. Supposedly she was director of the Canada Mission in the early '70s when the Maharaj Ji first came. Then it attracted a lot of druggies because Maharaj Ji was offering this psychedelic experience and yet it was organic. That is interesting enough how it is presented. You can get high without drugs and see the light without drugs. Well, anyway there are all these people coming together in the Mission, a lot of weird people and a lot of straight people. Maharaj Ji was in Canada for a program and another pre-

mie in the States hung himself in one of the ashrams. This deprogrammer who had been co-director of the ashram called Maharaj Ji and told him a brother just killed himself. "Maharaj Ji," she said, "a lot of premies are freaked out. You know what's going on?" And his response, in a very detached way was, "It's okay, just meditate; it's okay, don't worry about it." The way she described the situation, I could see how he would do that because actually I don't know if he is capable of anything else. He might go up on a stage in a very interesting outfit and say, "I'm God," but when it comes to dealing with people on a practical basis, it has to be dealt with eventually. You can't run away forever. That struck me and it made an impact because what I saw of Maharaj Ji, what I heard from this other premie, I could see how that would be possible.

Various other respondents, including members of Divine Light Mission, Hare Krishna, and a number of charismatic Christian groups, affirmed the important influence of former group members with regard to separation from the religious leader. While their influence was not in any way comparable to a coerced deprogramming situation, the converts reported many long hours of discussions with each other, recalling incidents of abuse and disappointment and assuring one another that they were doing the right thing in leaving. A former Hare Krishna devotee spoke directly to this issue:

My wife and I talked it over all the time. At first every day and then every week. We would keep talking about what happened to us and we had friends close by who quit with us and we would talk with them too. We had a support group and all of us were going through the same thing—just total anxiety when we left.

A large part of the anxiety over separation derives from the dislocating effects of leaving a world of total meaning and the protection and security of the omnipotent father. At this stage of the disaffection process, devotees experience a competing set of needs as the desire for autonomy conflicts with the longing to reestablish bonds with the charismatic leader. As feelings of anger and resentment also begin to surface at this time, such feelings help the devotee to disengage from the guilt and fears that continue to confuse ego boundaries and thus prevent total separation.

Anger in the Aftermath of Disaffection

The importance of anger in the disaffection process raises the question of controversial findings in the study of post-involvement attitudes and reactions. Both Levine (1984) and Wright (1984) minimize the significance of anger among religious converts who have left alternative movements, preferring to focus on what they have determined is the more common response to past commitment, that is, the overall feeling among followers that they do not regret their experience and in fact have become "wiser" because of their commitment.

In Wright's survey of post-involvement attitudes among 45 former devotees, only 7 percent reported feelings of anger while 67 percent believed that they were wiser for the experience. In the study presented here, the findings show some major differences. In this research, 55 percent of the respondents discussed feelings of anger and resentment immediately following their disaffection, but of these devotees, 90 percent reported that over time their anger dissipated and they were later able to assess their involvement with the group from a more positive perspective. The following excerpt from an interview with a Divine Light follower illustrates this shift in attitude:

> Sometimes I feel what an incredible waste and then other times I feel there was a real benefit to my being in. There are some things that I learned which are very beneficial. I was really bitter for a while and the counselor told me that I needed to go through my anger, through the hate. I've come through it. Basically what I feel is that there were a lot of emotions that were subdued all those years so that when they come up it is really an intense feeling. When I felt those things before, even last year, I would immediately do Holy Name or something to try to keep it down. In a lot of ways there is a lot of readjusting but it's also very exciting. I have a friend who is a former premie and he says every once in a while he has a soft spot for Maharaj Ji. I don't feel that way. I don't have a hard spot. I don't hate him so much any more.

The anger expressed by this devotee reflects what many others also felt, an intense rage in the months immediately following their separation.

As in the case of the abused child, anger allows the devotee to detach from the charismatic leader by replacing feelings of love and devotion with feelings of resentment and anger, thus making separation possible, although painful and distressing. Through the anger, the former convert establishes emotional distance from the leader, a distance which provides the necessary groundwork for redefining one's self apart from the association with the godlike figure. Only then is the individual ready and willing to integrate his religious experience into his or her new life outside the movement in an affirmative way. In the other two studies cited, it is not clear how long after separation the post-involvement attitudes of former converts were assessed. Perhaps their findings reflect a stage of disaffection in which the earlier and more negative emotional responses had already been worked through by the devotee, with the discrepancy in findings a function of time rather than a difference in emotional reaction.

If the initial phase of disaffection can be understood as a period of grief and adjustment in which guilt, fear, and anger are experienced by the devotee, then perhaps the second stage of separation can be viewed as the reintegration phase wherein the devotee acclimates to his or her new independent status through the adoption of a more positive world view in which the future is deemed exciting while the past is perceived as a valuable but painful lesson in life's disappointments. At this juncture in deconversion, reestablishing social and emotional ties outside the movement becomes the focus for meeting needs unfulfilled by the religious experience.

Reintegration and the Reestablishment of Social Roots

The reintegration phase of disaffection seems to be marked by a change in attitude toward the charismatic leader. Having acknowledged the loss, the anger, and the fear of separation, the devotee can once again consider the positive attributes of the leader and the essential goodness of the religious teachings, but now with the critical perspective of one who is aware of the dangers as well as the rewards of commitment. The reorientation of feelings and attitudes toward a more positive assessment of the experience contributes to a sense of relief as the former devotee begins to focus on the reality of separateness and the meaning of independence in terms of freedom rather than guilt and fear. This freedom is felt in all aspects of the devotee's life, including freedom from the religious discipline, freedom from the pressure to conform, freedom from the emotional demands of devotion, and freedom from the constraints of a narrowly defined sense of self. As one former convert expressed this change:

> Now that I am not a member, I feel much freer, under much less pressure. I don't feel the sense of someone trying to lay a guilt trip on me for some things I don't consider wrong. I'm not talking about sleeping around or anything like that. I'm talking about smoking cigarettes or marching for gay rights. I have freedom to think and explore without the fear of being shunned.

Goffman (1961) describes similar moments of freedom when an inmate experiences life outside the institution:

> Of course, immediately upon release the inmate is likely to be marvelously alive to the liberties and pleasures of civil status . . . the sharp smell of fresh air, talking when you want to, using a whole match to light a cigarette. . . . (1961:71)

Both the inmate and the convert savor the privileges of a nonrestricted life.

As freedom replaces guilt and fear as the emotional focus of deconversion, the former devotees begin to engage in social interactions which lead to reintegration and the establishment of new social ties. Of the variety of settings in which new social bonds may be formed, the four which are most prevalent for disaffected group members are school, work, family, and another religious movement. Each of these social environments provides a connection to the world outside the religious group and a link to an alternative social reality on which to base a reassessment of self.

Over half the respondents in this study entered college or some vocational training program soon after their separation from the group. In this regard, school provided new social relationships, alternative world views and intellectual perspectives, and training for occupations and professional employment that could replace the former involvement with the religious community. For those devotees who were employed outside the religious movement before their departure, the work setting provided an opportunity for alternative social interactions and a redirecting of interests and thoughts away from the religious movement.

A focus on family and marital relationships provided another source of reconnection. In this regard, the emotional fulfillment once associated with the leader was sought through the relationship to a spouse, lover, or child. In comparatively few cases, and these were among the younger devotees, parents and siblings were the source of redirected needs fulfillment. More commonly, converts who had married or had established love relationships while still a follower turned to these relationships to cope with the feelings of loss associated with the charismatic leader. Here a former Divine Light disciple describes the birth of his child soon after he left the movement:

> I saw my child being born, that incredible love, that power taking a human form. I started looking at that reality. This power was real, the spirit, whatever I was worshipping became real at that moment and I didn't have to put it on Maharaj Ji. This was real life and real power.

Other followers spoke of that same sense of reality and tangibility as they transferred their devotion and love to spouse or child, the persons in their lives who were constant, who reciprocated their feelings, and whose relationship was not based on a promise of unconditional spiritual love, but on a day-to-day experience of emotional involvement and response.

The return to the nuclear family is thus one response to deconversion among disaffected devotees who were as yet unwilling to relinquish the family ideal. In an interesting reaction to disillusionment with the religious communities and their patriarchal leaders, converts sought refuge in the creation of their own family structures in an attempt to once again live out the idealism associated with middle-class American life. The return to the nuclear family on the part of religious devotees was facilitated by the emergence of the conservative political and social climate which has characterized the 1980s. As a greater emphasis has been placed on traditional family values and the importance of religion, converts to new religious movements discovered that the ideals for which they had joined these groups were now compatible with the restructuring of familial norms in the outside world. Thus, in their transition to a secular life the former devotees could take their place alongside others of their generation whose lives now reflected the desire for stability and security within the circumscribed world of the primary family.

Yet what distinguished the religious converts from others of their generation was the desire to retain both spiritual and familial ideals through the continued commitment to a religious path. The final setting in which social roots were established after disaffection was a new religious movement. The tendency toward reconversion has been discussed in the previous chapter with respect to the importance of seeking out a replacement for the loss of the charismatic leader and the primal object of love that he represents. In this continual search for the convergence of love and spirituality, converts appear to be engaged in a developmental process as described by Robert Balch and David Taylor (1978), wherein the goals of ideological and spiritual growth are valued in themselves as the individual is engaged in a process of spiritual seeking, remaining open to new ideas and alternatives. A significant shift, however, appears to take place after disaffection as former converts seek out new religious associations that allow for a greater separation between the attainment of family goals and the fulfillment of spiritual objectives.

Although the quest for spirituality does not seem to be lost among disaffected devotees, the desire to sacrifice one's self so completely for the goal of spiritual knowledge is reevaluated in light of past experience. Among the 40 respondents who participated in the study, not one spoke of atheism in response to their disillusionment, and few expressed an interest in returning to mainstream religion which, according to the majority of respondents, had previously failed to meet their spiritual needs. The evidence strongly suggests that those who choose a spiritual path in life will stay on that path, even if it is hurtful, troubling, and disappointing. The desire for spirituality and religious meaning is not easily extinguished; the death of one god leads to the search for another.

7.

Conclusion

This research offers a study of deconversion that examines the social and psychological bonding to the religious group and the ways in which such bonds are severed in the process of disengagement from the movement. At the outset of the analysis, conversion was explained from the perspective of the social construction of reality; the devotee enters a world of total meaning in which his or her subjective reality is modified by the group through the adoption of a specific world view, a basic belief system, and the notion of deification as it is associated with the charismatic leader. As this new social reality is formed around group membership, bonds to the organization and to the leader of the religious community are developed within a familial context that replicates the bonds of childhood.

As the development of socio-emotional bonds to the movement is a defining characteristic of conversion, membership in the group is contingent upon conformity, dependence, and obedience, particularly in the relationship between the devotee and the charismatic leader. Through conversion, the leader becomes the manifestation of God on earth. The discovery of this idealized god-figure offers the promise of complete and total gratification, the merging of love and spirit in a single relationship to one who is perceived as unique in his purity and blessed in his relationship to immortality. The willingness to follow, to become an obedient and self-sacrificing devotee, can be understood as a desire for wholeness, the drive toward perfection of the human condition that can only be achieved through the bond to the charismatic leader. The dependency and conformity thus exhibited by religious devotees is a reflection of a power dynamic in which the leader is perceived as the sole source of emotional satisfaction and spiritual knowledge.

The power that the religious leader maintains over his devotees is further enhanced by the social environment of religious movements. The hierarchical arrangements of the group power structure, the rigid moral codes, the authoritarian religious philosophy, and the demands of spiritual practice are designed to discourage notions of personal equality and self-responsibility. Through intense indoctrination, norms of conformity and control are established which reduce ambiguity surrounding the existence of God. In effect, the proof of God's existence, as it is manifested in the leader, relies on the strong beliefs of group members and the acceptance of a doctrine of faith which cannot be challenged.

To achieve this goal of total acceptance, initiates are encouraged to see themselves in childlike relationship to the charismatic figure as he assumes the responsibilities of parenting: love, discipline, guidance, and knowledge. Because conversion often results in childlike dependency, the loss of autonomy experienced by the devotee is similar to childhood, in which the convert looks to a significant other to structure and to place constraints on his or her life. For the younger devotees, the assumption of dependent status is often an extension of family relationships, while for others, especially the older and more experienced converts, conversion might be considered as the continual search for a childhood security that has never been realized.

The patriarchal family structure that characterizes new religious movements represents an important aspect of contemporary conversion as devotees seek to discover an ideal family in which a spiritual father is present whose loving and gentle caretaking fulfills the needs left unmet by traditional patterns of patriarchal child rearing. The desire for the paternalistic bond among religious converts is a manifestation of a cultural system in which strong emphasis is placed on family values and the role of the authoritative father as provider and protector. As such, the growth of charismatic movements over the past two decades can be interpreted in part as the failure of the family to provide an emotionally supportive environment in which the father assumes an instrumental role in the affective development of the child and creates a secure refuge from the outside world.

Within this perspective on conversion, deconversion becomes another form of failed idealism, this time within the context of the religious family that has replaced the family of origin as the source of primary socio-emotional relationships. Confronted with the reality of conflict and the manipulation of power within the religious community, the religious convert must now come to terms with the failure of yet another familial ideal. In so doing, the devotee attempts to resolve the ambivalence surrounding the desire to leave and the desire to stay as separation from the movement signifies a transition toward autonomy. Within this analytical framework, departure from religious movements involves a complex process of breaking and reforming bonds which takes place through social and psychological exit from the group. A three-stage model representing this process of changing commitment is shown below:

A Model of Deconversion from Nontraditional Religious Movements

Figure 1 presents a model that traces the stages of deconversion as these have been elaborated throughout the analysis of data. While the various steps in each stage have been presented in a strict linear fashion, this is not to suggest that all cases of deconversion proceed along the exact sequential path developed here. In 80 percent of the cases in this study, however, ties to the group were severed before ties to the leader, and the phases of disaffection generally conformed to the steps outlined below.

Stage I: Severing Ties to the Religious Group

In the first stage of disaffection, the devotee exercises his or her autonomy in a challenge to the social constraints of group commitment. Thus the first step toward independence is rejection of an authority structure that seeks to control the social relations of group members, a safer and less dramatic course of action than a direct challenge to the leader and perhaps to God. This rejection of the bureaucratic authority within the movement, the hierarchy of power that creates an intermediary link between the disciples and the charismatic figure, is most frequently manifested in violating social rules and regulations. In the transition from obedience to insubordination, the devotee expresses disillusionment with the religious bureaucracy, an authority that had previously been accepted as both legitimate and valid.

Stage II: Severing Ties to the Charismatic Leader

Total disaffection, the second stage of deconversion, is achieved when autonomy from the leader as well as from the group has been accomplished. Because this is a more difficult and painful step to take, just a little over half (57%) of the respondents in this study had reached this point of independence at the time of their interview. The relationship between the leader and follower is defined by intense love and devotion that tends to obscure the boundary between self and other. The result of such bonding is that the devotee begins to see him or herself primarily in relation to a charismatic figure who assumes the responsibility for fulfilling the affective as well as the spiritual needs of the individual. Thus, the leader is internalized as the idealized patriarchal God to whom complete surrender is given.

Once such commitment is experienced, the loss of autonomy that is suffered is not easily regained. The process of separation might therefore be viewed as a redress in the balance of power; the individual struggles with a desire to remain connected to a relationship in which one individual is perceived as the source of unconditional love and spiritual knowledge. Because of the power attributed to the charismatic authority, it is possible to understand the desirability of entering into a subordinate relationship with the religious leader and to appreciate the way in which dependency can be created, sustained, and maintained even under conditions of subservience, exploitation, and cruelty.

In order to relinquish this object of primal love, one who offers the promise of religious truth and certainty, the devotee must experience extreme disillusionment with the leader. Such disillusionment takes place over time as doubts and unmet expectations contribute to a growing restlessness with the leader's inability to meet the demands made of the omnipotent father, the tender lover, and the spiritual godhead. As the leader exhibits disturbing human qualities of greed, selfishness, anger,

Figure 1. Model of Deconversion from Nontraditional Religious Movements

STAGE 1. Severing Ties to the Religious Group

1. *Dissatisfaction*	2. *Conflict*	3. *Disillusionment*	4. *Separation*	5. *Alternative Social Bonds*	
Rules and regulations imposed by the religious hierarchy interfere with fulfillment of social needs (friendship, love, intimacy, and so on).	Devotees conflict with authority structure over the regulation of social life, spiritual demands, and status issues.	Conflict over control of social and spiritual life results in disillusionment with the power structure, the religious organization, and the peer group.	Separation from the group redresses the balance of power in favor of personal autonomy.	Alternative social bonds are sought to replace those to the social group (see also Stage III: Initial Separation).	PARTIAL DISAFFECTION STATE

STAGE II. Severing Ties to the Charismatic Leader

1. *Dissatisfaction*	2. *Disillusionment*	3. *Doubt*	4. *Challenge to Authority*	5. *External Reinforcement*	6. *Rejection of the Leader*	
Actions of the leader (abuse, rejection, spiritual betrayal) are inconsistent with his role as spiritual figurehead and loving parent.	Devotees experience feelings of disappointment, hurt, and disillusionment with the leader as a result of his actions.	The reality brought to bear by the leader's actions casts doubt on his true spirituality and connection to god.	Devotees become less willing to accept the authority of the leader as his power base is diminished by the loss of spiritual credibility.	Outside ties (former devotees, friends, family) reinforce the critical perspective in which the leader is now viewed.	Rejection of the leader and his world view redresses the balance of power in favor of individual initiative and the reestablishment of identity.	TOTAL DISAFFECTION STATE

STAGE III: Complete Separaion from the Movement and the Redefinition of Social Reality

1. *Initial Separation*	2. *Period of Mourning*	3. *Emotional Readjust-ment*	4. *Reintegration*	
Devotees experience isolation and loneliness as a result of the loss of religious identity and social affiliation.	Devotees enter a period of emotional strain in which anger, guilt, and fear accompany their sense of isolation.	Following the period of mourning, a more positive view of the former religious commitment emerges which is accompanied by a sense of freedom and desire to redefine one's self apart from the religious identity.	The reestablishment of social and religious roots outside the movement contributes to the reconstruction of social reality and the reestablishment of a separate ego identity for the former devotee.	TOTAL DECONVERSION

and brutality, his actions provide both a catalyst and reinforcement for ultimately rejecting the charismatic authority, a severing of emotional ties which leads to a choice of self over other.

The evolution from faithful devotee to questioning disciple is marked by developing doubts and a more critical approach to the leader's authority and his teachings. In the early phases of separation, the devotee experiences internal psychological pressure to remain, as well as overt external pressure from other group members with whom he or she still associates. It is, however, the internal anxieties and fears associated with asserting one's independence through the rejection of God that troubles disaffected converts most. Feelings of connectedness, unification, and wholeness engendered by the charismatic leader are powerful ties that influence the struggle for autonomy as these spiritual goals are experienced within a theology of absolutism. The rigid and authoritarian structure associated with the world of total meaning defines one true path to God and immortality. In challenging the belief system and the leader's rightful authority, the devotee risks losing God's love and the punishment of damnation. To achieve psychological separation through the restoration of clearly defined ego boundaries the devotee must redefine the leader as human, not God, and thus redefine him or herself as an individual apart from a mortal being who had once been deified.

Final separation is rarely accomplished without another source of spiritual identification to whom the devotee can transfer his or her affection and more importantly his or her understanding of the spiritual aspects of human existence. For, as this study indicates quite strongly, the desire to explore and to understand the spirit, the part of consciousness that is linked to the nonmaterial and thus nonrational source of life, remains a strong motivation among those who seek a religious world view, even when this world view has proven to be a false and deceptive path to truth.

Stage III: Total Separation from the Movement and the Redefinition of Social Reality

The final departure from the religious movement, as it is manifested in the redefinition of social reality and the adoption of a new self-concept by the devotee, seems to be contingent upon the availability of spiritual as well as social alternatives to replace the bonds of the prior religious commitment. Social alternatives such as family, school, and work provide a social context and stimuli through which a new social identity may be created. Simultaneously, other religious movements provide alternative spiritual affiliations that tend to be less authoritarian and demanding of their followers. Thus, the move toward independence and autonomy is a gradual process as the disillusioned devotee seeks to satisfy religious and spiritual goals without the sacrifice of self that characterized the former commitment.

The experience of disillusionment suggests that religious devotees do not seek independence as a goal in itself, but remain in search of a balance between connection and autonomy. Total freedom brings with it the fear of alienation, isolation, and loneliness; complete dependency, on the other hand, eliminates the exercise of control over one's life, the ability to make choices, and the possibility of an existence that is not tied to validation by another. Neither human condition is optimal and so the struggle ensues throughout life and throughout relationships, whether they be intimate, marital, parental, or religious, to find that balance between freedom and commitment, love of self and love of other. In this regard, the religious devotee is no different from any other individual who, in search of the idealized relationship, discovers that there is no such thing as unconditional love. Rather, every form of commitment has certain demands that limit freedom; as such demands become excessive, the faith and belief in the ideal are increasingly difficult to maintain and may ultimately be shattered.

Finally, the significance of idealization evident in both the acceptance and rejection of charismatic authority can only be understood within the context of the social construction of ideals. Throughout this analysis it has been maintained that the nature of contemporary religious commitment is shaped by the culture of patriarchy. Through the internalization of the paternal ideal the father becomes the symbol of masculine power who embodies the standards of human ethical behavior and the moral laws by which members of a society judge themselves (Mitchell, 1974). When this ideal is projected on to the person of the charismatic leader, the apparent contradictions in his behavior challenge the supremacy of a male-defined ethical system and point to a failure of patriarchy to actualize the masculine ideal. Thus, the shattering of idealism that is associated with the deconversion process represents more than a disillusionment with "corrupt leadership." At the deepest levels of commitment and love, rejection of the spiritual father symbolizes the failure of a morality that is grounded in the theology of dominance and control.

References

Anderson, M. L. (1983). *Thinking About Women: Sociological and Feminist Perspectives*. New York: Macmillan.

Bainbridge, W. S., & Stark, R. (1979). Cult Formation: Three Compatible Models. *Sociological Analysis*, 40(4), 283-95.

Balch, R. W., & Taylor, D. (1978). Seekers and Saucers: The Role of the Cultic Milieu in Joining a UFO Cult. In J. T. Richardson (ed.), *Conversion Careers: In and Out of the New Religions* (pp. 113-28). Beverly Hills/London: Sage Publications.

Balint, M. (1965). *Primary Love and Psycho-Analytic Technique*. New York. Liveright Publishing Corporation.

Beckford, J. (1976). Explaining Religious Movements. *International Social Science Journal*, 29, 23-39.

Bellah, R. (1976). The New Religious Consciousness and the Crisis of Modernity. In C. Glock & R. Bellah (eds.), *The New Religious Consciousness* (pp. 333-52). Berkeley: University of California Press.

Berger, P. (1985). *The Goddess Obscured*. Boston: Beacon Press.

Berger, P. L. (1979). *Facing Up to Modernity*. New York: Basic Books.

Berger, P. L., & Luckmann, T. (1966). *The Social Construction of Reality*. New York: Doubleday.

Bergmann, M. S. (1971). Psychoanalytic Observations on the Capacity To Love. In J. B. McDevitt & C. F. Settlage (eds.), *Separation-Individuation* (pp. 15-40). New York: International Universities Press.

Blau, P. (1964). *Exchange in Social Life*. New York: John Wiley & Sons, Inc.

Bromley, D. G., & Shupe, A. D. (1979). *"Moonies" in America: Cult, Church, Crusade*. Beverly Hills/London: Sage Publications.

Bromley, D. G., & Shupe, A. D. (1980). Financing the New Religions. *Journal for the Scientific Study of Religion*, 19(3), 227-39.

Bucher, G. R. (1983). Worlds of Total Meaning. *Soundings*, 64(3), 274-85.

Budapest, Z. (1986). *The Holy Book of Woman's Mysteries*, Volumes 1 and 2. Oakland, Calif.: Susan B. Anthony Cover No. 1.

Burgess, R. L., & Nielsen, J. M. (1974). An Experimental Analysis of Some Structural Determinants of Equitable and Inequitable Exchange Relations. *American Sociological Review*, 3, 427-43.

Chodorow, N. (1974). Family Structure and Feminine Personality. In M. Rosaldo & L. Lamphere (eds.), *Woman, Culture, and Society* (pp. 43-66). Stanford, Calif.: Stanford University Press.

Chodorow, N. (1978). *The Reproduction of Mothering*. Berkeley: University of California Press.

Clark, J. (1978). Cults. *Journal of the American Medical Association*, 242(3), 279-84.

Cohen, A. (1955). *Delinquent Boys*. Glencoe, Ill.: Free Press.

Contratto, S. (1987). Father Presence in Women's Psychological Development. In J. Rabow (ed.), *Advances in Psychoanalytic Sociology: A Text and Reader* (pp. 139-55). Melbourne, Fla.: Krieger.

Conway, F., & Seigelman, J. (1978). *Snapping: The Epidemic of Sudden Personality Change*. New York: J.B. Lippincott.

Culpepper, E. (1978). The Spiritual Movement of Radical Feminist Consciousness. In G. Baker and J. Needleman (eds.), *Understanding New Religions* (pp. 220-34). New York: Seabury Press.

Daly, M. (1975). *The Church and the Second Sex*. New York: Harper & Row.

Downton, J. F. (1973). *Rebel Leadership: Commitment and Charisma in the Revolutionary Process*. New York: Free Press.

Downton, J. F. (1979). *Sacred Journeys: The Conversion of Young Americans to Divine Light Mission*. New York: Columbia University Press.

Downton, J. F. (1980). Theory of Sequential Development of Spiritual Commitment. *Journal for the Scientific Study of Religion*, 19, 382-94.

Edwards, C. (1981). The Dynamics of Mass Conversion. *Marriage and Family Review*, 4, 31-41.

Emerson, R. (1962). Power Dependence Relations. *American Sociological Review*, 27, 31-41.

Emerson, R. (1969). Operant Psychology and Exchange Theory. In R. Burgess & D. Bushell (eds.), *Behavioral Sociology* (pp. 380-405). New York: Columbia University Press.

Enroth, R. (1977). *Youth, Brainwashing and the Extremist Cults*. Grand Rapids, Iowa: Zondervan.

Festinger, L. (1957). *A Theory of Cognitive Dissonance*. Evanston, Ill.: Row Peterson.

Freud, S. (1960). *Group Psychology and the Analysis of the Ego*. New York: Bantam Books.

Freud, S. (1950). *Totem and Taboo*. New York: W. W. Norton.

Garbarino, J., Guttman, E., & Seeley, J. (1986). *The Psychologically Battered Child*. London: Jossey-Bass Publishers.

Gergen, K. (ed.) (1980). *Social Exchange*. New York: Plenum Press.

Gerth, H., & Mills, C. W. (1946). *Max Weber: Essays on Sociology*. New York: Oxford University Press.

Gimbutas, M. (1982). Women and Culture in Goddess-Oriented Old Europe. In C. Spretnak (ed.) *The Politics of Women's Spirituality* (pp. 462-69). New York: Anchor Books.

Glock, C. (1976). Consciousness among Contemporary Youth: An Interpretation. In C. Glock & R. Bellah (eds.), *The New Religious Consciousness* (pp. 353-66). Berkeley: University of California Press.

Glock, C. (1964). The Role of Deprivation in the Origin and Evolution of Religious Groups. In R. Lee & M. E. Marty (eds.), *Religion and Social Conflict* (pp. 24-36). New York: Oxford University Press.

Goffman, E. (1961). *Asylums*. New York: Doubleday.

Graves, R., & Patai, R. (1964). *Hebrew Myths: The Book of Genesis.* New York: McGraw-Hill.

Hagglund, T. B. (1982). A Psychoanalytic Study on Background in Religion. *Scandinavian Psychoanalytical Review*, 5, 137-48.

Hardy, R., & Cull, J. (1974). *Creative Divorce.* Springfield, Ill.: Charles C. Thomas.

Hershell, M., & Hershell, B. (1981). Our Involvement with a Cult. *Marriage and Family Review*, 4, 131-40.

Holbrook, D. (1967). *Object Relations.* London: Methuen & Co.

Homans, G. (1961). *Social Behavior: Its Elementary Forms.* New York: Harcourt Brace Jovanovich.

Hood, R. W., Jr., & Hall, J. R. (1980). Gender Differences in the Description of Erotic and Mystical Experiences. *Review of Religious Research*, 21, 195-207.

Irwin, J. (1970). *The Felon* (pp. 108-130). Englewood Cliffs, N.J.: Prentice-Hall.

Jacobs, J. L. (1984). The Economy of Love in Religious Commitment: The Deconversion of Women from Nontraditional Religious Movements. *Journal for the Scientific Study of Religion*, 23(2), 155-71.

Jacobs, J. L. (1987). Deconversion from Religious Movements. *Journal for the Scientific Study of Religion*, 26(3), 294-307.

Jacobs, J. L. (1989). The Effects of Ritual Healing on Female Victims of Abuse: A study of empowerment and transformation. Forthcoming in *Sociological Analysis.*

Jacobs, R. (1971). Emotive and control groups as mutated new American utopian communities. *Journal of Applied Behavioral Science*, 2.

Kim, B. S. (1979). Religious Deprogramming and Subjective Reality. *Sociological Analysis*, 40(3), 197-207.

Kohut, H. (1971). *The Analysis of Self.* New York: International University Press.

Krippendorff, K. (1980). *Content Analysis.* Beverly Hills/London: Sage Publications.

Kübler-Ross, E. (1970). *On Death and Dying.* New York: Macmillan.

Leidig, M. (1982). *Violence against Women.* Unpublished paper, presented 1982.

Lerner, G. (1986). *The Creation of Patriarchy.* New York: Oxford University Press.

Levine, S. (1984). *Radical Departures: Desperate Detours to Growing Up.* New York: Harcourt Brace Jovanovich.

Lofland, J., & Stark, R. (1965). Becoming a World Saver: A Theory of Conversion to a Deviant Perspective. *American Sociological Review*, 30, 862-74.

Lofland, J. (1978). Becoming a World Saver Revisited. In J. T. Richardson (ed.), *Conversion Careers: In and Out of the New Religions.* Beverly Hills/London: Sage Publications.

Long, T. E., & Hadden, J. K. (1983). Religious conversion and the concept of socialization: Integrating the brainwashing and drift models. *Journal for the Scientific Study of Religion*, 3, 1-15.

Marx, J. H., & Ellison, D. L. (1975). Sensitivity training and Communes: Contemporary Quests for Community. *Pacific Sociological Review*, 18(4), 442-60.

Mauss, A. L. (1979). Dimensions of Religious Defection. *Review of Religious Research*, 10, 128-35.

Mitchell, J. (1974). *Psychoanalysis and Feminism*. London: Allen Lane.

Needleman, J., & Baker, G. (eds.) (1978). *Understanding New Religions*. New York: Seabury Press.

Newman, W. (1974). *The Social Meanings of Religion*. Chicago: Rand McNally College Publishing Company.

Niebuhr, H. R. (1929). *The Social Sources of Denominationalism*. New York: Henry Holt & Co.

Pagels, E. (1981). *The Gnostic Gospels*. New York: Vintage Books.

Parsons, T., & Bales, R. (1955). *Family, Socialization, and Interaction Process*. Glencoe, Ill.: Free Press.

Patrick, T. (with Tom Dulack) (1977). *Let Our Children Go*. New York: Dutton.

Pollock. G. H. (1975). On Mourning, Immortality and Utopia. *Journal of American Psychoanalytic Association*, 23, 334-62.

Reich, A. (1953). Narcissistic Object Choice in Women. *Journal of American Psychoanalytic Association*, 1, 22-44.

Richardson, J. T. (ed.) (1978). *Conversion Careers: In and Out of the New Religions*. Beverly Hills/London: Sage Publications.

Richardson, J. T., & Stewart, M. (1978). Conversion Process Models and the Jesus Movement. In J. T. Richardson (ed.), *Conversion Careers: In and Out of the New Religions*. Beverly Hills/London: Sage Publications.

Robbins, T., & Anthony, D. (1972). Getting Straight with Meher Baba: A Study of Drug-Rehabilitation, Mysticism and Post-Adolescent Role Conflict. *Journal for the Scientific Study of Religion*, 11(2), 122-40.

Robbins, T. (1977). Cults and the Therapeutic State. Unpublished paper.

Robbins, T., Anthony, D., Doucas, M., & Curtis, T. (1976). The last civil religion: Reverend Moon and the Unification Church. *Sociological Analysis*, 36(2), 111-25.

Robbins, T., Anthony, D., & Richardson, J. (1978). Theory and Research on Today's New Religions. *Sociological Analysis*, 39(2), 95-122.

Robbins, T., & Anthony, D. (1978). New Religions, Families, and Brainwashing. *Society*, 15(4), 77-82.

Robbins, T., & Anthony, D. (1982). Deprogramming, Brainwashing, and the Medicalization of Deviant Religious Groups. *Social Problems*, 29(3), 283-97.

Robbins, T. (1988). Transformative Impact of the Study of New Religions. *Journal for the Scientific Study of Religion*, 27(1), 12-31.

Ross, N. (1975). Affect as Cognition with Observations on the Meaning of Mystical States. *International Review of Psychoanalysis*, 2, 79-94.

Rubin, L. B. (1983). *Intimate Strangers: Men and Women Together*. New York: Harper & Row.

Ruether, R. R. (1972). *Liberation Theology*. New York: Paulist Press.

Ruether, R. R. (1977). *Mary: The Feminine Face of the Church*. Philadelphia: Westminster Press.

Ruether, R. R. (1985). *Womanguides: Readings Toward a Feminist Theology*. Boston: Beacon Press.

Ruth, S. (1980). *Issues in Feminism*. Boston: Houghton Mifflin.

Schaef, A. (1981). *Women's Reality*. Minneapolis: Winston Press.

Schmidt, M. G. (1981). Exchange and Power in Special Settings for the Aged. *International Journal of Aging and Human Development*, 14(3), 157-66.

Sennett, R. (1970). The Brutality of Modern Families. *Transaction*, 7, 29-37.

Shaffer, R. (1982). Spiritual Techniques for Re-powering Survivors of Sexual Assault. In C. Spretnak (ed.), *The Politics of Women's Spirituality* (pp. 462-69). New York: Anchor Books.

Shapiro, E. (1977). Destructive cultism. *American Family Physician*, 15(2), 80-83.

Simmonds, R. B. (1978). Conversion or Addiction: Consequences of Joining a Jesus Movement Group. In J. T. Richardson (ed.), *Conversion Careers: In and Out of the New Religions* (pp. 113-28). Beverly Hills/London: Sage Publications.

Singer, J. (1976). *Androgyny*. New York: Doubleday.

Skonovd, L. N. (1981). *Apostasy: The Process of Defection from Religious Totalism*. Ph.D. dissertation. Ann Arbor, Mich.: University Microfilms International.

Smith, A. (1978). Black Reflections on the Study of New Religious Consciousness. In G. Baker and J. Neddleman (eds.), *Understanding New Religions* (pp. 220-34). New York: Seabury Press.

Solomon, T. (1981). Integrating the "Moonie" Experience: A Survey of Ex-members of the Unification Church. In T. Robbins and D. Anthony (eds.), *In Gods We Trust: New Patterns of Religious Pluralism in America*. New Brunswick, N.J.: Transaction.

Spretnak, C. (ed.) (1982). *The Politics of Women's Spirituality*. New York: Anchor Books.

Starhawk (1979). *The Spiral Dance: A Rebirth of the Ancient Religion of the Great Goddess*. San Francisco: Harper & Row.

Stone, M. (1976). *When God Was a Woman*. New York: Dial Press.

Strauss, R. (1976). A Situation of Desired Self-change and Strategies of Self-transformation. In J. Lofland (ed.), *Doing Social Life* (pp. 252-72). New York: John Wiley & Sons.

Streiker, L. D. (1974). *Mind-bending: Brainwashing, Cults and Deprogramming in the '80s*. Garden City, N.Y.: Doubleday & Company.

Thorne, B. (ed.) with M. Yalom (1980). *Rethinking the Family: Some Feminist Questions*. New York: Longman.

Tipton, S. M. (1982). *Getting Saved from the Sixties*. Berkeley: University of California Press.

Toch, H. (1965). *The Social Psychology of Social Movements*. New York: Bobbs-Merrill Co.

Travisano, R. (1970). Alternation and Conversion as Qualitatively Different Transformations. In G. P. Stone & M. Garverman (eds.), *Social Psychology Through Symbolic Interaction* (pp. 594-606). Waltham, Mass.: Gihn Blaisdell.

Umansky, E. (1985). Feminism and the Reevaluation of Women's Roles within

American Jewish Life. In Y. Haddad and E. Findly (eds.), *Women, Religion, and Social Change* (pp. 477-94). Albany: State University of New York Press.

Underhill, E. (1955). *Mysticism: A Study in the Nature and Development of Man's Spiritual Consciousness*. New York: Meridian Books.

Ungerleider, J. T., & Wellisch, D. K. (1979). Coercive Persuasion (Brainwashing), Religious Cults, and Deprogramming. *American Journal of Psychiatry*, 136 (3), 279-82.

Walker, B. G. (1983). *The Woman's Encyclopedia of Myths and Secrets*. San Francisco: Harper & Row.

Wallace, R., & Wolf, A. (1980). *Contemporary Sociological Theory*. Englewood Cliffs, N.J.: Prentice-Hall.

Wallis, R. (1978). Recruiting Christian manpower. *Society*, 15(4), 72-74.

Wallis, R. (ed.) (1982). *Millennialism and Charisma*. Belfast: The Queen's University.

Weiss, F. R. (1963). Defection from Social Movements and Subsequent Recruitment to New Movements. *Sociometry*, 26(1), 1-20.

Weiss, R. S. (1975). *Marital Separation*. New York: Basic Books.

Wilber, K. (1981). *Up from Eden*. Boulder, Colo.: Shambhala Press.

Wilson, B. (1982). *Religion in Sociological Perspective*. New York: Oxford University Press.

Wiscombe, J. (1983, September 11). Chogyam Trungpa Rinpoche holds court in Boulder. *Focus Magazine, Sunday Daily Camera*, pp. 3-9.

Wright, S. A. (1984). Post-involvement Attitudes of Voluntary Defectors from New Religious Movements. *Journal for the Scientific Study of Religion*, 23(2), 172-82.

Wright, S. A. (1983). A Sociological Study of Defection from Controversial New Religious Movements. Ph.D. dissertation, University of Connecticut.

Wright, S. A., & D'Antonio, W. (1980). The Substructure of Religion: A Further Study. *Journal for the Scientific Study of Religion*, 19, 292-98.

Appendix A

1. When did you first become involved with this religious group?
2. How long were you a member?
3. When did you leave the group?
4. Can you tell me a little about how you first became involved? Did you have friends in the group or had you heard of the movement some other way?
5. Tell me a little about your experience while a member of the group.
6. What changed for you, what prompted you to leave?
7. Did your decision to leave have anything to do with what was taking place in your life outside the movement (career, education, family, friends, and so on)?
8. How long did you consider leaving before actually making the break?
9. Was it a difficult decision to make?
10. What difficulties did you encounter in leaving (pressures to stay from group; personal attachments; feelings of ambivalence)?
11. Was your family supportive of your leaving the group (and of your entering the group)?
12. What kind of support did you get after you left—family, friends, and so on?
13. Do you ever feel as if you would like to return to the group again?
14. How is your life changed now that you are no longer a member?
15. Do you think you would ever join another religious movement again?

Appendix B

1. Of which religious group were you a member? _____
2. How long were you affiliated with the group? _____
3. At what age did you first become involved? _____
4. How would you describe your position within the movement? (Check all that apply.) ___ devotee ___ teacher ___ administrator ___ worker ___ other (specify)
5. Did you contribute financially to the religious movement? _____
   If so, indicate to what extent. _____
6. While you were a member, did you live within the religious community or apart on your own? _____
7. Are you now a member of another religious movement? _____
   If so, please specify. _____
8. What is the religious background of your childhood? _____
9. What is your present level of education? _____
   What was your educational level at the time you entered the group? _____
10. What is your current occupation? _____
    Is it the same occupation you held while you were a member of the religious group? _____ If no, please indicate what your occupation was then.
11. Are you (check one) ___ married ___ divorced ___ single ___ living with someone
12. Do you have any children? ___ If yes, how many? _____
13. Please indicate ___ Female ___ Male
14. What is your present age? ___

If you need more space for any of the questions, use the reverse side.

Index

Abuse: in Buddhism, 96; in charismatic Christianity, 92–93, 94, 97; by charismatic leaders, 97, 98; in Divine Light Mission, 94, 96; in Sikhism, 96; in Tantric Buddhism, 94–95
Alternative religions. *See* Nontraditional religions
Androgyny (Singer), 82
Anger, and deconversion, 119–20
Anne (Sikh disciple): background of, 50–51; dissatisfaction and disillusionment of, 51–52, 53; reconversion of, 51, 52, 54. *See also* Sikhism
Anthony, Dick, 2–3, 8
Arvi Coshi, 106

Bahai, 45–46, 98. *See also* Greg (Bahai leader)
Balch, Robert, 123
Battering. *See* Abuse
Berger, Pamela, 83
Berger, Peter, 2–3
Blacks, in charismatic religions, 5
Brainwashing, 40*n*. *See also* Nontraditional religions
Bromley, David, 66
Bucher, G. R., 39
Buddhism: abuse in, 96; authoritarianism of, 49; characteristics of, 27; control in, 102; deconversion from, 114; status positions in, 56; time commitment to, 49; Vajra directors of, 42. *See also* Karmapa (Buddhist leader); Kathy (Buddhist disciple); Robert (Buddhist disciple); Seth (Buddhist disciple); Tantric Buddhism

Charismatic Christianity: abuse in, 92–93, 94, 97; deconversion from, 71, 112, 113, 115–16; deprogramming in, 118; dissatisfaction and disillusionment with, 97–98, 106; familial nature of, 92; patriarchal authority in, 92; sex roles in, 65, 68–69, 70, 87, 97; shunning in, 113. *See also* Cheryl (charismatic Christian); Christian Fellowship; Church of Christ; Pastor Jim (charismatic Christian)
Charismatic leaders: abuse by, 97, 98; authoritarianism of, 73, 105; bonding with, 77, 78–79, 81, 86–88, 89, 90, 100–101, 105, 111, 118, 124, 127, 130; dependency on, 13, 104, 124, 125, 127; dissatisfaction and disillusionment with, 96–97, 98–99, 101–102, 103, 104, 117, 118, 127, 128, 130, 131; exoneration of, 72; as god figures, 73–74, 76, 80, 84, 86, 90, 91, 97, 101, 103, 104, 106, 108, 116, 117, 120, 124, 125, 127, 130; as human figures, 91–92; as idealized self, 73, 77, 78, 84; inconsistencies of, 92, 101, 102, 127, 130, 131–32; love for, 75; lovelessness of, 100; materialism of, 102; omnipotence of, 76, 124, 127; as patriarchal authorities, 13, 73, 76–77, 78, 79, 80, 84, 86, 89, 107, 108, 115, 116, 118, 122, 125, 127, 131–32; redefinition of, 130; and reintegration, 120; replacement objects for, 103–104, 105–106, 123, 130, 131; subordination to, 75, 127; women as, 105. *See also* Charismatic religions